Routledge Guides to the

The Routledge Guidebook to Wollstonecraft's *A Vindication of the Rights of Woman*

"Bergès beautifully explicates *A Vindication of the Rights of Woman* in the context of the western philosophical canon. It is a sophisticated and graceful reading of the text."

Natalie Taylor, *Skidmore College*

A Vindication of The Rights of Woman is one of the most influential works of the eighteenth century. In what is considered by many to be one of the earliest feminist texts, Mary Wollstonecraft argues that women should be given more rights at a time when 'equality' was usually reserved for men.

The Routledge Guidebook to Wollstonecraft's A Vindication of the Rights of Woman explores:

- The political and philosophical climate in which A Vindication of the Rights of Woman was published
- The key ideas and themes which Wollstonecraft developed in the text
- The enduring influence of Wollstonecraft and her classic work

This Guidebook is ideal for readers coming to *A Vindication of the Rights of Woman* for the first time and anyone who wants to know more about Wollstonecraft's revolutionary ideas and their impact.

Sandrine Bergès is Assistant Professor of Philosophy at the University of Bilkent, Turkey.

ROUTLEDGE GUIDES TO THE GREAT BOOKS

Series Editor: Anthony Gottlieb

The Routledge Guides to the Great Books provide ideal introductions to the work of the most brilliant thinkers of all time, from Aristotle to Marx and Newton to Wollstonecraft. At the core of each Guidebook is a detailed examination of the central ideas and arguments expounded in the great book. This is bookended by an opening discussion of the context within which the work was written and a closing look at the lasting significance of the text. *The Routledge Guides to the Great Books* therefore provide students everywhere with complete introductions to the most important, influential and innovative books of all time.

Available:

Forthcoming:

Routledge Guides to the Great Books

The Routledge Guidebook to Wollstonecraft's *A Vindication of the Rights of Woman*

Sandrine Bergès

LONDON AND NEW YORK

To my husband, Bill Wringe, who introduced me to Wollstonecraft, and to our daughter, Charlotte Wringe, the youngest feminist philosopher I know.

First published 2013
by Routledge
2 Park Square, Milton Park, Abingdon, Oxon OX14 4RN

Simultaneously published in the USA and Canada
by Routledge
711 Third Avenue, New York, NY 10017

Routledge is an imprint of the Taylor & Francis Group, an informa business

British Library Cataloguing in Publication Data
A catalogue record for this book is available from the British Library

Library of Congress Cataloging in Publication Data
Berges, Sandrine.
The Routledge guidebook to Wollstonecraft's A vindication of the rights of woman / Sandrine Bergès.
p. cm. -- (The Routledge guides to the great books)
Includes bibliographical references (p.) and index.
1. Wollstonecraft, Mary, 1759–1797. Vindication of the rights of woman. 2. Women's rights--Great Britain. 3. Women--Education--Great Britain. I. Title.
HQ1596.B47 2013
323.3'40941--dc23
2012014839

ISBN: 978-0-415-67415-7 (hbk)
ISBN: 978-0-415-67414-0 (pbk)
ISBN: 978-0-203-09418-1 (ebk)

Typeset in Garamond
by Taylor & Francis Books

MIX
Paper from
responsible sources
FSC® C004839
www.fsc.org

Printed and bound in Great Britain by the MPG Books Group

CONTENTS

ACKNOWLEDGMENTS

I would like to thank James Alexander, Istvan Aranyosi, Piers Benn, Marianne Berges, Tony Bruce, James Caudle, Anne-Marie Chaput, Anca Gheaus, Lena Halldenius, Gokcenur Hazinedar, Banu Helvacioglu, Calum Neill, Mark Nelson, Linda Nicholson, Karen Stohr, Barry Stoker, Tom Stoneham, Natalie Taylor, David Thornton, Lucas Thorpe, Roberta Wedge, Simon Wigley, Jonathan Wolff, Bill Wringe, Colin Wringe, the participants of the Bilkent Philosophy work-in-progress seminar, the participants of the 2010 conference on Women's Political Thoughts in Europe during the Enlightenment, and its organizers, Karen Green, Lisa Curtis-Wendlandt and Paul Gibbard, for help, advice, feedback and encouragement on various aspects of this project.

SERIES EDITOR'S PREFACE

"The past is a foreign country," wrote British novelist, L. P. Hartley: "they do things differently there."

The greatest books in the canon of the humanities and sciences can be foreign territory, too. This series of guidebooks is a set of excursions written by expert guides who know how to make such places become more familiar.

All the books covered in this series, however long ago they were written, have much to say to us now, or help to explain the ways in which we have come to think about the world. Each volume is designed not only to describe a set of ideas, and how they developed, but also to evaluate them. This requires what one might call a bifocal approach. To engage fully with an author, one has to pretend that he or she is speaking to us; but to understand a text's meaning, it is often necessary to remember its original audience, too. It is all too easy to mistake the intentions of an old argument by treating it as a contemporary one.

The *Routledge Guides to the Great Books* are aimed at students in the broadest sense, not only those engaged in formal study. The intended audience of the series is all those who want to understand the books that have had the largest effects.

AJG
October 2012

AUTHOR PREFACE

Mary Wollstonecraft was a political philosopher of the Enlightenment, a period which ran roughly throughout the eighteenth century, and which claims thinkers as diverse as Locke, Voltaire, Kant, Hume, Adam Smith, Rousseau and Condorcet. Although other women took part in the debates of that period, the quality and the quantity of Wollstonecraft's published works, as well as the fact that her writings were influential at the time they were published, make her a clear and obvious candidate for a list of great thinkers of the Enlightenment. One hopes that her presence in that list will eventually encourage philosophers to include other women writers in what is known as *the canon*, that is, the group of texts that are understood as definitive of our culture and civilization, and that constitute the reading list for any undergraduate course of study in a particular discipline, in this case, in philosophy. Wollstonecraft's *A Vindication of the Rights of Woman* is possibly the clearest example of why her work is so valuable. As well as being a classic of Enlightenment philosophy, it is probably the earliest sustained philosophical argument for gender equality in English. And although nowadays feminist thinkers may well take issue with some of the views Wollstonecraft develops in that book, it is nonetheless the case that we owe an immense debt to her pioneering work. For that reason alone, we should read *A Vindication*.

There are of course other reasons. *A Vindication* is an important part of the Enlightenment project. Not that the Enlightenment was a project – those who were engaged in it did not necessarily think of themselves as part of a research team engaged in solving a common problem. But at least, towards the end of the eighteenth century, writers exchanged views often via correspondence and the publication of pamphlets, which included translations between the main European languages. These writers also seemed to be engaged in similar philosophical pursuits. These pursuits were in part theoretical – debates on the nature and role of reason, both as what makes us essentially human and as a tool for acquiring knowledge; and in part practical – the application of the principles of the Enlightenment to the pursuit of better political arrangements. Wollstonecraft's work played a significant part in both. By arguing that reason cannot be truly universal if it is gendered, she rectified some inconsistencies in thinkers such as Kant and Rousseau, who defended a similar vision of a universal reason while at the same time claiming that female reason was different in quality as well as quantity. But her part in the practical side of the Enlightenment is perhaps more significant. While Rousseau, Kant and others were busy preparing the intellectual ground for the liberation of French men from the oppression of the monarchy, Wollstonecraft was concerned with freeing the other half of the French nation, and indeed, of any nation, from the oppression of men. While Hobbes and Locke had tried to redefine what it meant to be a subject in a state, Wollstonecraft was pointing out that no state could be either just or properly functioning that excluded from citizenship half of its adult inhabitants, and that citizenship did not cease to exist inside the home. She was by no means the first person to point this out, but because she was part of a group of radical political thinkers, and because she wrote and published as much as any of her male peers, her thoughts were perhaps more significant, and in any case more influential. Of course, belonging to the right set does not in itself bestow significance on an author, but what it does is give that author the opportunity, the means and the confidence to write, and to develop her ideas as a response to the ideas of others. Wollstonecraft's works, even though they presented ideas that were rare, if not unique in that time, were not isolated: they were part of a debate, making use of concepts and arguments that were recognized. Her works were, in fact, a significant part of an ongoing dialogue on rights, freedom and equality.

If Wollstonecraft's works were part of the canon, I would not be writing this book. It would have been written long before. Or else I would be attempting to justify the need for writing yet another philosophical introduction to *A Vindication*. But although some very good philosophical commentaries on *A Vindication* have been published in recent years, none of them is really introductory. They support research rather than teaching. My aim is to produce a book that will be useful to students taking a philosophy course of which Wollstonecraft's *A Vindication of the Rights of Woman* is a part, and for teachers who are considering teaching such a course. My aim is twofold. On one hand, I want to talk the reader through the main arguments of the text, chapter by chapter, analysing them, engaging with them, sometimes making the context to which she was responding more explicit. But also, I aim to show how Wollstonecraft's arguments are relevant in any context, using contemporary issues to discuss their application. Of course, that means looking at twentieth-century feminist responses to Wollstonecraft; but mostly it means showing that her philosophical reflections can shed light on contemporary problems, in the same way that we sometimes appeal to Kant, or Mill, to discuss issues in global justice. Studying Wollstonecraft has more than simply historical value. Like other important philosophers of any period or place, she is providing us with tools we can use to conduct our own investigations, solve our own problems. I will be offering a few examples of how she might be useful to us.

1

THE FIRST OF A NEW GENUS

THE LIFE OF MARY WOLLSTONECRAFT

On 10 September 1797, at the age of thirty-eight, Mary Wollstonecraft died in London of puerperal fever, ten days after giving birth to her second daughter, Mary. She died painfully, as the result of an infection brought on, probably, by the use of unsterilized medical instruments. She left behind two daughters, newborn Mary, and Fanny, aged three, born from a relationship to a previous lover, Gilbert Imlay.[1] Wollstonecraft also left behind her husband of six months and lover for a year, the moral philosopher William Godwin, two *Vindications* – on the rights of men (1790) and women (1792) – a semi-autobiographical novel, *Mary*, three educational books, some translations, a large number of book reviews in the *Analytical Review*, a book on the French Revolution, written during a stay in France between 1792 and 1795, a published volume of letters from Sweden, Denmark and Norway, and some unpublished works including the unfinished novel *Maria or the Wrongs of Woman*.

To have achieved that much writing in such a short time, while also bringing up a child single-handedly and providing

emotional and financial support for several members of her extended
family, she would have to have been a singularly energetic, talented
and hard-working woman. And by all accounts, she was. The
portrait we have of Wollstonecraft's life, from her widower's memoirs and from her own letters, is one of a very driven individual, who
fought back conventions and relative poverty to establish herself,
first as a an educated woman whose opinion on current affairs and
philosophical debates mattered, and second as a successful professional writer. But we should not imagine that she was always
single-minded and concentrated on her work. Like many human
beings, she spent a significant portion of her life obsessing over
failed love affairs, twice even to the point of attempting suicide.
Her letters tell us that she was not above wasting time on pettiness
either. She seemed to spend a fair amount of time whining to her
sisters about how hard her life was. She complained of how
unpleasant the jobs she had taken on to support them were, or
how hard it was to beg loans from rich friends. She complained of
her health too, suffering from headaches and stomachaches that frequently prevented her from working.[2] She was, however, robust, as
became evident from her ease through pregnancy and childbirth.[3]
One might venture that her health problems were stress-related,
induced by constant worry about whether she would have enough
money to support herself and her dependents, and discomfort at her
almost unique situation as an independent, unmarried middle-class
woman who took it upon herself to have a literary career and be
the head of her family.

Between the ages of nineteen and twenty-seven, Wollstonecraft
took on a series of jobs, at first to gain independence from her
parents, then out of necessity to support herself, her sisters,
brothers and extended family. At the age of nineteen, she left
home to work as a lady's companion in Bath, hoping to make
enough money to rescue her family from her father's increasing
debts. She came home after a little over a year to nurse her sick
mother, and was with her until her death a year later. She then
founded a school in Islington (and then in Newington Green)
thereby creating a home and an income for herself, her sisters and
her close friend Frances Blood. As this was not sufficient to pay
for the debts she and her sisters accumulated through the failing

schools, Wollstonecraft went to work as a governess for an aristocratic family in Ireland, from which position she was dismissed
a year later. When, at the age of twenty-eight, she came back
from Ireland to London, her friend and editor of her first book,
Thoughts on the Education of Daughters (1787), suggested she might
earn a living by writing. He offered her a job as a writer on
the *Analytical Review*, of which he was the editor, and encouraged
her to write more books. Wollstonecraft wrote to her sister:
'Mr. Johnson ... assures me that if I exert my talents in writing,
I may support myself in a comfortable way. I am then going to be
the first of a new genus – I tremble at the attempt.'[4]

Wollstonecraft was not, of course, the first woman ever to make
money from writing. There were at the time a large number of
educational treatises and children's books written by women, and
for which women were paid. Women were also paid for reviews,
novels and translations. There was nothing terribly unusual about
a woman making money from writing.[5] But Wollstonecraft was not,
like many of the others, a woman peddling manuscripts in the hope
of making a little money: she had a job. Johnson guaranteed her a
decent income if she would take on commissions from him. She
was a staff writer, and a journalist, in charge of regular reviews. In
this, she was indeed probably the first.

Nothing in Wollstonecraft's background predisposed her for a
philosophical career. Many of her contemporaries who had achieved
some sort of literary or scientific success either came from rich or
intellectual backgrounds, or married into them. Wollstonecraft's
family was middle class and very undistinguished. Her father was
an alcoholic and a gambler who had lost any chance the family
had of being comfortable or even respectable. Her mother was the
victim of domestic abuse, and perhaps because of that, had very
little time to devote to the education of her daughters. She seems
not to have wasted much love or affection on them either, preferring her oldest son. Wollstonecraft seems to have regarded her
both as a victim to be defended, and an example of bad parenting
to be avoided.

Unlike some other 'neglected' daughters, Wollstonecraft did
not have the run of big libraries in which she could educate herself
while no-one was watching.[6] She relied on friends to lend her

books, to advise her in her readings, and to engage her in intellectual discussions about them. During her Yorkshire adolescence, it was her best friend Jane Arden's father, a philosopher by profession, who provided her with a library and guidance in her readings, and in her early twenties, the Revd and Mrs Clare in Hoxton, London, and the friend she met through them, Frances Blood, were responsible for much of her reading as well for her developing writing skills.

Her own intellectual thirst guided her to seek out these people's friendships. Other than that, she had access to very little learning. She knew no Greek or Latin, and taught herself French and German later on, so that she could become a governess and so that she could take on translation work, but found it very difficult.[7] In her mid-twenties, Wollstonecraft was befriended by Mrs Burgh, widow of the director of a dissenting academy, and influential author James Burgh.[8] Mrs Burgh would become her patron for several years, setting her up in Newington Green, at the time a village a couple of miles out of London, helping her find a house and pupils for her school there and rescuing her when she needed money. Mrs Burgh introduced her to the Newington Green community of Rational Dissenters, and in particular to Richard Price, a Welsh dissenting preacher who, thanks to his writings on economics, was on friendly terms with the government, but who was also adviser to the founding fathers of the United States of America. Price was also active in the anti-slavery movement, a staunch republican, and a defender of the French Revolution. He played an important part in shaping Wollstonecraft's career, first by lending her books, discussing them with her and introducing her to the publisher Johnson. But his influence went further: it was a sermon given by Price on the French Revolution that prompted Edmund Burke to write his *Reflections on the Revolution in France*, in which he defended the rights of the aristocracy and denounced what he saw as the excesses of the Revolution, predicting that it would end in a bloodbath. Burke's pamphlet was also, in many ways, a personal attack on Price and on his republican beliefs. Two people immediately rose in defence of their friend Price. One was Thomas Paine, with his *Rights of Man*. But Wollstonecraft beat him to publication with her own *A Vindication of the Rights of Men*, which she wrote in six weeks.

Rational Dissenters were, for the most part, republicans who favoured equality and sometimes had strong views on slavery, women and education. Wollstonecraft's time in Newington Green helped her become a radical thinker. It also developed her education. Dissenters were not allowed to enter English universities (Oxford or Cambridge, at the time), and so Newington Green, home to many prosperous city merchants and bankers, had become some sort of a university village, rife with books and intellectual discussions. Wollstonecraft borrowed books from her new friends, and heard from them about those she could not read.[9]

When Wollstonecraft started to work for Johnson, she would have gained access to even more books – those she was asked to review, and those she could borrow. And she was a voracious reader. Somehow she would have done her best to catch up so that she could take part in debates over dinner at Johnson's place, with men such as the painter Fuseli, who had received a classical education, or Paine and Godwin, who, although they had not benefited from a university education either, would have found it easier as men to educate themselves. Of course, many books remained inaccessible to her as they were in Greek or Latin. Plato's works, for example, had not yet been translated, nor had the majority of Aristotle's. She would have picked up what she could in conversation, but remained very much an outsider in her lack of classical culture.

Throughout her short life, Wollstonecraft took on responsibilities that were traditionally male. She supported a number of people financially, including her sisters, at times two of her brothers, her friend Frances Blood's entire family, and a few others besides. In 1784 she arranged for one of her sisters, Elizabeth, who was possibly going through a kind of postnatal depression, to leave her husband, whom she had come to hate and fear. Together the sisters ran away, and lived in hiding for some time until they could figure out what to do. It was to provide for her sisters, that Wollstonecraft decided to set up a school for girls. But it was also to further her own dream of living and working together with her friend Frances Blood, who joined Wollstonecraft and her sisters as a teacher. The dream was short-lived, as Frances married and moved to Portugal, and shortly afterwards died in childbirth. Wollstonecraft travelled to Portugal to help, but was powerless, and grieved for a long time afterwards. After that, the second school failed and Wollstonecraft took up a job as a governess in Ireland in order to pay her debts. Before leaving for Ireland, Wollstonecraft had given Johnson the manuscript for her *Thoughts on the Education of Daughters*, based on her own experience as a woman and as a teacher of girls. Her ideas were influenced by those of the Dissenters – Revd Burgh, her patron's late husband, had written a treatise on education in which he took up and responded to some of Locke's ideas on that topic. Wollstonecraft's book was a continuation of that debate.[10] When Wollstonecraft came back from Ireland, Johnson offered her a job.

In 1792 the artist Fuseli, another of Johnson's friends, disappointed Wollstonecraft by not being in love with her. The two had been close friends, but Fuseli was married and had no interest in their friendship developing in the way she was hoping. Unhappy, she decided to move to Paris, by herself, to observe and document the Revolution.[11] She had intended to go before, with the Fuselis, but that trip had been aborted for reasons of security. She decided to go anyway. Wollstonecraft stayed in France for three years, writing and meeting with members of the Revolution. It was in Paris that she met the American businessman Gilbert Imlay. They became lovers and had a child. Although Imlay registered Wollstonecraft as his wife with the American Embassy, and she took his name when a state of war was declared between Britain and France and things became difficult for the English in Paris, they were never married.

The affair did not last after Paris. When Wollstonecraft returned to London in 1795, it became apparent that Imlay was tired of her, and she attempted suicide. To raise her spirits (and possibly to ensure she was out of the way), Imlay sent her on a mission. A sea captain had absconded with a cargo of silver belonging to him. The ship had disappeared somewhere in Scandinavia. Imlay needed someone to go and look for it, and to talk with his lawyers in Denmark. He sent Wollstonecraft, armed with a power of attorney, her baby daughter, and a French maid. She found out some information, defended Imlay's interests with gusto, and at the same time produced a volume of letters describing the natural wonders of

Scandinavia, its political arrangements, and the lives of the people she met there. The letters were published on her return and received excellent critical reviews.

Shortly after her return from her Scandinavian expedition, in February 1796, Wollstonecraft met with Godwin. The two had met previously, at Johnson's table, but had not got on very well. This time they did, and in August they became lovers. In December, Wollstonecraft was pregnant, and in March 1797, she married Godwin. She had no desire to risk her reputation and lose her friends by having another child so very obviously out of wedlock.[12] It was bad enough that she would have to acknowledge that she had never been married to Imlay, but that might pass off, she thought, provided she married Godwin. Both wished to preserve their independence, and even after marriage, maintained separate quarters. A few months later, baby Mary was born at home. Because the placenta was not ejected during the birth, it had to be pulled out. During the (painful) process, an infection was introduced. After ten days of suffering, she died.

In some ways, Wollstonecraft's outlook on life had been fairly conventional: despite her living in close quarters with Dissenters, and marrying an atheist, Wollstonecraft remained staunchly religious all her life, and preferred the Anglican church. She did, it seems, flirt with the French revolutionary approach to religion, which was to replace God with the Supreme Being, remaining vague as to what the Supreme Being was supposed to be. Certainly, she did not believe in a god who was male, or had created men in 'his' image, and women from a rib bone. Her god was un-gendered, and above all rational. She did not hesitate to condemn passages in the Bible that pretended otherwise. But she did not see any of this as incompatible with a gentle Anglicanism. She and Godwin joked about their differences of opinion at her deathbed, which did not prevent him, in his memoirs, from presenting her as an atheist. This contributed greatly to Wollstonecraft's fall from public favour after her death. From being a popular, well respected author, she became a figure of ridicule and shame. This happened almost overnight after the publication of Godwin's memoirs of his wife.

Godwin wrote the memoirs immediately after his wife's death, perhaps as a sort of therapy, and to pay tribute to her. He decided, as was in keeping with his beliefs, to be perfectly honest about everything. He described her love affairs, her strong affection for her friend Fanny Blood, her unrequited passion for Fuseli, and her illegitimate affair with Imlay, as well as the fact that her first child, Fanny, was born out of wedlock. Some people knew this already, of course: it would not have been possible for Wollstonecraft to marry Godwin had she already been married to Imlay. But after the publication of the memoirs this became public knowledge, as did her two suicide attempts,[13] and the fact that she was Godwin's lover for several months before she became his wife.

The respected writer of educational books for girls, whose quirky political outlooks had, for the most part, been overlooked by the wider public, was no longer a respectable woman, and her books were not to be read:[14]

> Fierce passion's slave, she veer'd with every gust,
> Love, Rights, and Wrongs, Philosophy, and Lust.
>
> (Thomas J. Matthias in Gordon 2006: 371)

The scandal, followed closely by the puritanism of the nineteenth century, meant that Wollstonecraft was no longer taken seriously. When John Stuart Mill wrote 'The Subjection of Women', even though many of his arguments were the same as Wollstonecraft's, he did not refer to her.

A VINDICATION OF THE RIGHTS OF WOMAN

> One form of immortality is hers undoubtedly: she is alive and active, she argues and experiments, we hear her voice and trace her influence now among the living.
>
> (Woolf 1965/1932: 161)

In November 1789, Wollstonecraft's friend and mentor, the Dissenter clergyman Richard Price, gave a sermon in celebration of the anniversary of the Glorious Revolution of 1688, in which he praised the French Revolution and encouraged the English not to be satisfied with what they had achieved 100 years ago, but to keep fighting for their rights. One year later exactly, Edmund Burke published his *Reflections on the Revolution in France*, in which he denounced Price and the actions of the French Assembly. Burke had himself been a moderate republican, at least insofar as he supported American independence. But the 'proceedings in France', in particular the arrests of the king and queen by commoners, worried him deeply. He feared both for the political stability of England, were the revolutionary spirit to catch on, and for the loss of certain values that he held dear and that could survive only if there was an aristocracy: chivalry, sensibility, dignity. Without the 'decent drapery of life', he said, we would lose all reason to value each other, and particularly women, because without this drapery, 'a king is but a man; a queen is but a woman; a woman is but an animal; and an animal not of the highest order' (Burke 1968: 171). The publication of Burke's book gave rise to several replies from within dissenting and republican circles. The first of these was Wollstonecraft's *A Vindication of the Rights of Men*, published in the same month as Burke's book. A few months later came Catherine Macaulay's *Observations on the Reflections of the Right Hon. Edmund Burke, on Revolution in France*, and Thomas Paine's *Rights of Man*. The latter is the only one that is still widely read.

In 1790, Wollstonecraft had been working for Johnson for four years. She was becoming a more confident writer, making more money, and, dining once a week at Johnson's house with other radical writers and artists, she was a fully paid-up member of his intellectual circle. She had known Price for six years. It was he who had encouraged her to read more widely, and who had introduced her to Johnson. Price was then old and sick (he died a year later). His friends felt it was their duty to stand up for him, and Wollstonecraft was the first to do so. Her book is clearly a defence of her friend: 'In reprobating Dr Price's opinions', she tells Burke, 'you might have spared the man' (Wollstonecraft 1999/1790: 17). But she nonetheless presented a clear and convincing exposition of the argument for universal rights, and at the same time rebuked the value system so dear to Burke, that of 'sensibility'. The concept of 'sensibility' very much belongs to the eighteenth century – the wearing of one's emotions on the surface, the ability to be moved to tears by a beautiful flower or poem. 'Theatrical attitudes',

Wollstonecraft calls it, and 'the manie of the day' (*ibid*.: 6), a fake sort of compassion that really ought not to trump the concern that is due to fellow humans. The look of impotence on the king's face, or of fear on the queen's, should not weigh against the fact that people were starving, she argued. Her arguments in the first *Vindication* prepare the grounds for those of the second, in which she claims that a concern for sensibility is to blame for many of the prejudices that hold women down.

Wollstonecraft was already very aware, both as a woman and as a writer, of the depth of double standard that regulated relations between the sexes. As someone who was not afraid to speak her mind, she may well have discussed her views on this with her colleagues at the *Analytical Review*. In particular, when Catherine Macaulay's *Letters on Education* was published in 1790, Wollstonecraft was very struck by the historian's sensible and radical approach to the question of women's education. At this point someone, probably Johnson, may well have suggested to her that she write the second *Vindication*. This time, she took more than just a few weeks to write it. The first manuscript was completed in January 1792. The second came out in December, just as she was leaving for Paris.

After the publication of the first edition of the second *Vindication*, Wollstonecraft wrote to her friend Roscoe:

> I am dissatisfied with myself for not having done justice to the subject. – Do not suspect me of false modesty – I mean to say that had I allowed myself more time I could have written a better book, in every sense of the word ... I intend to finish the next volume before I begin to print, for it is not pleasant to have the devil coming for the conclusion of a sheet fore it is written.
>
> (Wardle 1979: 206)

We don't know the extent to which she was right to be dissatisfied, as the version of *A Vindication* that is now available is the revised edition, and she had had twelve months to revise the text then.[15] But this letter tells us something else. Not only did Wollstonecraft typically write in a hurry, but her works were published as pamphlets. That is, pages were printed as they were written, and the book was first sold cheaply, unbound, and later sold as a bound volume for a greater price (Pitcher 1975: 323). This explains her reference to the 'devil coming for the conclusion of a sheet fore it is written'. If the press was to be got ready at specific intervals, or specific times, the writer had to produce a sufficient number of pages. This may well explain also some of the variations in the quality of the writing that can be observed in Wollstonecraft's book, as well as the impression one sometimes gets of lack of overall planning for the book. In that respect, her work would be very different from that of Hume, say, or Kant, neither of whom was a hack writer or obliged, in order to keep their work, to produce a number of pages regularly, but could instead work at their own rhythms, planning, drafting, revising early chapters in the light of new ones, reorganizing the structure if needed.[16] Wollstonecraft, along with many other professional writers of her time, did not have that luxury. It is also perhaps relevant that, at the time she was writing the second *Vindication*, Wollstonecraft was experiencing romantic turmoils – her friendship with Fuseli turned into a crisis – and Johnson felt he had to push her to write in order to keep her from falling into depression. All in all, she was probably right to feel that the work needed to be thoroughly revised. In the eleven months after the publication of the first edition, she worked not only on correcting stylistic mistakes, but on strengthening the argument wherever she could. What she could not do, presumably, was revise the overall structure of the book. It had to be a second edition of the same book, not a completely different one. People who had invested in the first edition, or who had bought the pamphlets cheaply as they were being printed, should not be made to feel that they had wasted their money on a poor first draft. Wollstonecraft was in some way bound by this unsatisfactory first edition.

Despite her own dissatisfaction with the work, it was very well received. Her first *Vindication* had already received favourable reviews – the second received more, and sold well. This may come as a surprise, given that we do not expect the eighteenth-century public to have been that sympathetic to the idea of gender equality: after all, no-one read Wollstonecraft and granted women rights. But *A Vindication of the Rights of Woman* was not perceived as a political treatise on gender equality so much as a work on the reform of women's education. There were already a large number of books written on that topic, and it had become generally accepted that women's education, as it stood, needed reforming, and many of Wollstonecraft's suggestions struck people as eminently sensible – which they were. Even among the conservative, people did seem to agree with Wollstonecraft that women ought to be, first and foremost, healthy, and that they also had better not be fully occupied by frivolous activities. In fact, even the ultra-conservative Mary Astell, at the beginning of the eighteenth century, had been of the opinion that although women should obey their husbands in all things, they had better be well educated (Springborg 1997). What would have rattled her audience would have been the recognition that she meant to achieve what the title stated: namely vindicate women's rights. But this was obviously read by many as an attempt to vindicate women's rights to be educated, and not much else. The radical aspect of her work, her at times strident voice, were put down to her revolutionary sympathies, well recorded in her previous work, *A Vindication of the Rights of Men.* This, and in general her association with the Revolution, was not of itself problematic. Until the year of her death, it was still seen as almost respectable to be defending the French Revolution. Even the Terror was taken at first more as a sign that the French had not handled things well, than that there should not have been a revolution.

Nonetheless, where Wollstonecraft's work received bad press, it was for her revolutionary tendency rather than her feminism. Horace Walpole called Wollstonecraft 'that Hyena in Petticoats' as a response to her *View of French Revolution*, not her *Vindication*, which he had not read (Janes 1978: 294). The satire written by the neo-Platonist Thomas Taylor, *A Vindication of the Rights of Brutes* (Taylor 1792/1996), although it came out straight after the publication of *A Vindication of the Rights of Woman*, was aimed at ridiculing Wollstonecraft's republican arguments, along with those of Paine's, more than her feminist ones.

Wollstonecraft's feminist arguments, insofar as they went further than arguments about educational reform, were very clearly perceived by at least some readers, such as Mary Hays and Mary Robinson, who both went on to defend women's rights in their writings. Margaret Mount Cashell, who had been Wollstonecraft's favourite tutee in Ireland, attempted to live part of her adult life in accord with Wollstonecraft's principles. She first turned against her Anglo-Irish aristocratic background to defend Irish independence. Later, in Germany, having left her husband, Margaret Mount Cashell disguised herself as a man in order to attend lectures on medicine, following Wollstonecraft's advice that 'women may be physicians as well as nurses' (Gordon 2006: 403). Other women might have become aware of Wollstonecraft's teachings had her works remained popular for long enough. Unfortunately, six years after its publication, the second *Vindication* was no longer readable by any one who considered themselves to be respectable. Again, this was not related to the feminist content of the book, or indeed to the content of the book at all. The members of the public were put off reading it because revolutionary terms had fallen into disrespect, and also because Wollstonecraft herself, following the posthumous publication of her husband's memoirs, was no longer respectable. She was seen as a loose woman, and an irreligious one. Interestingly, those who did try to keep up her legacy did not attempt to combat these perceptions of her character, but rather embraced them. Percy Shelley, a great admirer of Wollstonecraft who taught her daughter Mary to read her books, thought of her as a proponent of free love (an interpretation he was very eager to share with his lovers, including Wollstonecraft's daughters and their step-sister Clare Clairmont). Throughout the nineteenth century, Wollstonecraft was ignored, or merely revived in order to draw out her sentimental misadventures, her unreciprocated love for the painter Fuseli, her abandonment by the American Imlay, her illegitimate child by him, her suicide attempts – Wollstonecraft was used as a warning of what could happen to a woman who let herself be ruled by passion. Only at the beginning of the twentieth century were her feminist arguments looked at again with philosophical interest by the likes of Emma Goldman and Virginia Woolf, women who struggled in their careers as writers or political activists, and who needed to look back on the arguments of their predecessor to take up the battle once more.

FROM THE ENLIGHTENMENT TO THE TWENTY-FIRST CENTURY: A FEMINIST JOURNEY?

It would be easy to assume, given the damage that was caused by Godwin's memoirs to her reputation, that Wollstonecraft was no longer read after her death, but this is not quite the case. She was discussed by women she had mentored, such as the writer Mary Hays and her old student Margaret Mount Cashell, as well as by her own daughters and their friends, the Romantic poets. But Wollstonecraft was also politically influential via Owen, the socialist and trade unionist who had apparently professed his admiration of *A Vindication* to Fanny Godwin (Gordon 2006: 422–23). Owen's follower William Thompson was almost certainly alluding to Wollstonecraft when he wrote to his friend and co-author Mrs Wheeler that he was 'Anxious that the hand of a woman should have the honour of raising from the dust that neglected banner which a woman's hand nearly thirty years ago unfolded boldly, in face of the prejudices of thousands of years' (Thompson 1825: vii).

But within another thirty years, Wollstonecraft was all but forgotten. In her review of Margaret Fuller's *Women in the Nineteenth Century*, in which she compares that work with Wollstonecraft's *A Vindication*, the novelist George Eliot notes that *A Vindication* had not been reprinted since 1796, and that it was now 'rather scarce'. This was in 1855, nearly fifty years after Wollstonecraft's death. Eliot records surprise at the work not being at all scandalous but instead rather dull:

> There is in some quarters a vague prejudice against the *Rights of Woman* as in some way or other a reprehensible book, but readers who go to it with this impression will be surprised to find it eminently serious, severely moral, and withal rather heavy.[17]

Eliot suggested that this, rather than moral disapproval, might be the reason why the work was no longer popular: the public simply did not fancy reading a difficult book if they did not have to.

That the Victorians did not read Wollstonecraft is not to say that they did not also attempt to deploy arguments like hers in defence of women's rights. The most famous example is perhaps the work of J.S. Mill, *The Subjection of Women*. This work was preceded by ten years by Harriet Taylor's 'The Enfranchisement of Women', published in the *Westminster Review* in July 1851.[18]

What is interesting about both Taylor's and Mill's works is that, although many of their arguments appear to be derived from Wollstonecraft, at no point do they refer to her. Mill refers to no-one, but Taylor does: she mentions the fact that great thinkers 'from Plato to Condorcet' have defended the rights of women (Taylor 1851: 16). At the same time, she mentions that it will come as a surprise to her readers that the people who were defending women's rights in America, organizing a convention and speaking at it, were women. Clearly, she expects it to be news that women themselves should come up with the arguments for their own emancipations and have the courage to defend them publicly. This suggests that either she had not read Wollstonecraft, or if she had, like the rest of her generation, she had not seen beyond the romantic drama that appeared to have been her life.[19] Yet many of the arguments both she and Mill present appear to be derived in some sense from Wollstonecraft. It is possible that her words then made an unconscious impression on the minds of those predisposed to take up the battle against the oppression of women, that even if they did not acknowledge her, somehow they carried on in the path she had begun.

A Vindication came back into favour at the end of the nineteenth century and the start of the twentieth with the Suffragettes, who perceived Wollstonecraft as the mother of feminism. In particular, Virginia Woolf in Britain and Emma Goldman in the United States made a concerted effort to bring Wollstonecraft back into the public eye, and to hold her up as the mother of feminism. But perhaps they were more concerned about her as a woman than as an author, and it is not clear that many more people read *A Vindication* as a result of this publicity.

The second wave of feminism was not so kind to Wollstonecraft, as women in the 1960s and 1970s did not take well to her sometimes paternalistic tone, or to her references to female nature and the importance of motherhood in a woman's life. The attitude on sex and love she records in *A Vindication* would have seemed a bit prim and constricted to women seeking liberation. Also, for those who saw the personal as political, it may have been hard to reconcile Wollstonecraft's appeal to rationality for women with what they saw as the aberrations of her personal life (Kaplan 2002: 254). Perhaps understandably, as they were also political activists, the influential thinkers of the second-wave feminist movement did not try very hard to understand and interpret Wollstonecraft's text in a more charitable way. Now that there is, at least in the developed world, somewhat less urgency in defending feminist principles,[20] we are more at leisure to understand them in more depth and detail, and this is what is happening in Wollstonecraft scholarship – we are again interested in what she had to say, not just in how we can use her. Not surprisingly, it turns out that more careful reading of the text also yields richer and more useful interpretations for the twenty-first-century feminist.

PLAN OF THE BOOK

This book is divided into nine chapters, including this introduction. The chapters follow Wollstonecraft's, although not on a one-to-one basis, as some of her (twelve) chapters are shorter than the others, and she does not always follow a very clear path herself. In each chapter I pick out one or two themes that I judge to be central to her argument. I offer an analysis of Wollstonecraft's treatment of those themes, highlighting any argument she uses in defence of her views. I also suggest how these themes, and Wollstonecraft's treatment of them, may be relevant to contemporary debates in moral and political philosophy.

In Chapter Two, I discuss the front matter of *A Vindication* – the title, the preface, the advertisement and an introduction. I argue that these short texts should lead us to regard *A Vindication* at least in part as a treatise on education. This is indeed how the book was perceived when it was published, but I suggest that it is not only a treatise on education as Wollstonecraft perceives education as the first vital step towards achieving gender equality. In this chapter, I spend some time setting these texts in their historical and philosophical context – the French Revolution, in particular its proposed educational reforms, and the Enlightenment, with its emphasis on the liberating role of reason.

In Chapter Three, I offer an analysis of the arguments presented by Wollstonecraft in her first three chapters, with particular emphasis on her view that reason must be un-gendered. I discuss several of her arguments for that central premise in *A Vindication*, and show how she applies her conclusions to two problems: the inconsistency she perceives in men's treatment of women, and her views on the alleged superiority of men. In both cases, Wollstonecraft is struggling to apply a reasoned argument against the tide of centuries-old customs and beliefs.

In Chapter Four, I take a step back from the chronology of this study to offer my views on the ethical theoretical background of *A Vindication*. I suggest that Wollstonecraft's moral philosophy is strongly Aristotelian, and offer evidence that this is the case. I show that her discussions of virtues such as chastity and modesty follow a typically Aristotelian pattern, in that she looks for vices of excess and deficiency, and identifies virtue with a kind of wisdom. I also highlight the importance of the concepts of habituation and perfectionism in her thought.

In Chapter Five, I apply the discussion of Wollstonecraft's ethical theory to her study of the state of womanhood in her Chapter Four. In particular, I look at her explanation of the phenomenon she describes as the degradation of women, or women's unwillingness to achieve independence. I compare and contrast Wollstonecraft's arguments with those of her contemporary, the French revolutionary Condorcet, and with nineteenth-century philosopher Mill, but show that Wollstonecraft's arguments are deeper and more convincing. At the end of the chapter, I suggest that her views could be taken to enrich twentieth-century economist and philosopher Amartya Sen's concept of adaptive preferences, and therefore are useful in dealing with issues in global justice.

In Chapter Six, I look at Wollstonecraft's responses to her contemporaries, male and female writers, on the subject of women's emancipation. This discussion is based on her Chapter Five, 'Animadversions', but discusses only some of the writers she chooses to take on there. By adding some names of my own to Wollstonecraft's 'Animadversions', I also take this opportunity to situate her more fully within twentieth- and twenty-first-century feminist thought.

Chapter Seven focuses on Wollstonecraft's Chapter Six, and discusses her apparently ambiguous attitude to social mores and customs. On one hand, she finds concepts such as 'reputation' highly dangerous, and deems them responsible for much of what is wrong with her contemporaries' lifestyles, but on the other, she seems to be defending the need for taste and manners rather intransigently. I attempt to explain this ambiguity by relating it to her Aristotelian ethical bent. Good manners, I suggest, is a virtue for Wollstonecraft. Therefore it needs to be exercised in alliance with wisdom, not ignorance, and corresponding vices of excess and deficiency must be avoided.

Chapter Eight discusses *A Vindication*'s Chapters Nine to Eleven and, like them, focuses on the topics of love, marriage and family. It is in these chapters that Wollstonecraft approaches the question of actual rights – under the guise of discussing independence in marriage. I therefore pay particular attention to Wollstonecraft's arguments for the need for independence within marriage and the family. Her discussions of good and bad parenting are also relevant to this issue, insofar as Wollstonecraft believes that a good parent fosters the independence of their children, whereas a bad one is more likely to have recourse to blind authoritarianism.

In Chapter Nine, I discuss the final two chapters of *A Vindication*, and in particular the concrete proposal for educational reform Wollstonecraft is offering. I focus on the progressive aspects of this proposal, but also note a worrying tendency in these final chapters to talk about women's essential nature, and to make comments about motherhood, in particular, which might not be compatible with modern feminist thought.

2

THE RIGHTS OF WOMAN AND NATIONAL EDUCATION

READING THE FIRST PAGES

In this chapter I focus on the front matter of *A Vindication of the Rights of Woman*, a small but crucial number of pages consisting of three texts – the Preface, the Advertisement to the reader, and the author's Introduction. These texts give us important clues as to what we should expect to find in *A Vindication* and, just as importantly, what we should not expect to find. The main surprise is the Preface, a dedication to the Marquis de Talleyrand, in which Wollstonecraft presents her work not as a defence of women's rights, as the title indicates, but more particularly as a proposal for educational reform.

The title of the book, *A Vindication of the Rights of Woman*, of course, leads us to expect that the book will be about rights, and in particular about equality of rights between men and women, or at least granting women more rights. The title was probably inspired by the title of her previous work, *A Vindication of the Rights of Men*, which she wrote as response to Burke's *Reflections on the Revolution in France* – Thomas Paine's *Rights of Man*, published shortly after Wollstonecraft's is the better known reply to Burke. Both Paine and Wollstonecraft defended the Revolution from republican and egalitarian perspectives. Both argued that tyranny is always bad, and that it was legitimate for the French to revolt against their king, claim their freedom and their rights, and attempt to create a more egalitarian world.

Wollstonecraft went on to write *A Vindication of the Rights of Woman* with a mind to follow up on the success of the first *Vindication* by writing up her many thoughts on women's condition. But most of what she had previously written about concerned the education of women, rather than straightforward rights. So it should not be terribly surprising if her work on the social injustices that her contemporaries face concerns mostly educational reform.

Wollstonecraft does, however, clearly intend to say something more substantial about rights. The – very short – Advertisement warns the reader that there is more to come. It tells us that whereas the author had intended to cover everything in one volume, she has since realized that she would need a second volume to cover 'particular investigations', especially 'the laws concerning women' (Wollstonecraft 1999/1792: 69). There is very little elsewhere in the book to hint at what may or may not have been planned for that second volume, except in Chapter Nine, in which she reiterates that she has plans to discuss laws regarding women in a future work (*ibid.*: 226).

As it turns out, this future work was never written – considering Wollstonecraft died a mere five years after the publication of this first volume, and that in the interim she moved to France to write about the Revolution, took a trip to Sweden and Denmark, and had two children, this is maybe not surprising.[1] She did, however, write an unfinished novel, *Maria or the Wrongs of Woman*, considered by some to be the sequel to *A Vindication*.[2] In that work she offers a critique of women's legal situation, the fact that they have no right over their own person, no property right, and no legal entitlement to bring up their own children. The heroine, Maria, is a woman who, having run away from a bad marriage and an abusive husband, finds herself forcibly detained in a lunatic asylum, her property confiscated, and her child taken away from her. She befriends a servant who has been raped, then thrown out on the street with no alternative to prostitution to stay alive. This could well be seen as 'particular investigations' into 'the laws concerning women'. But the philosophical text does not discuss any of this. So what we are left with is a treatise on women's rights that hardly discusses the law at all.

In her Introduction, Wollstonecraft warns us that she is not going to discuss questions of equality between the sexes in too much detail either. She starts off with a reflection on the apparent inferiority of women and an observation that this is almost certainly due to 'a variety of concurring causes' originating from the partiality of society towards men. But she then goes on to reassure that she does not 'mean violently to agitate the contested question respecting the equality or inferiority of the sex' (72). Men are physically stronger, she tells us, and that is that.

This dismissal of the question of gender equality is deceptive, of course, and it can be interpreted in at least two ways – either as the thought that men's superiority is obvious and should not be questioned, or, more subtly in the context of her reassurance, that men's superiority consists only in physical strength, and that in every other respect men and women are equals. Simply as a commercial proposition, this caution makes sense. One has to remember that *A Vindication* was first published in pamphlet form, so that someone who did not like the first instalment would not buy the rest of the book. So it is understandable that in her Introduction, before she has started putting forward her arguments, the tools she will use to convince, she simply does not wish to scare off customers.

Wollstonecraft is, however, less gentle with some readers. She tells us outright that she is interested in addressing middle-class women rather than aristocrats, giving the distinct impression that she regards the latter as a lost cause.[3] And she sternly admonishes her female readers for possibly expecting to be flattered by the author – no, Wollstonecraft tells them that she will treat them as rational beings, not fragile, fascinating creatures. The Introduction is thus a warning, and an apology for the content to come. But it is more than that, as it also announces one of the fundamental principles of *A Vindication*, namely that women are rational beings and that their reasoning skills are subject to improvement in exactly the same way as men's. This will be the topic of the fourth section of this chapter. But for an accurate description of the contents of the book, it is perhaps better to turn to the Preface, the Letter to Talleyrand. In that text, unlike in her Introduction, Wollstonecraft specifies rather clearly what the agenda of *A Vindication* is supposed to be, and that agenda is not what one might expect from the title, or even from reading the first few chapters.

Talleyrand was an important figure of the French Revolution. He met Wollstonecraft in February 1792, while visiting London in his (unofficial) capacity as a peacemaker. Wollstonecraft was then engaged in preparing the second edition of *A Vindication*. An ex-clergyman (who had never really officiated) and a diplomat who served under Louis XVI, during the Revolution (apart from a brief period of exile to America), and through a succession of emperors and kings until his death under Louis-Philippe in 1848, Charles Maurice de Talleyrand-Perigord had a crucial role in shaping the ethos of the revolution. One of the writers of the Declaration of the Rights of Man, he was made responsible, in 1791, for the Convention's report on Public Instruction. The report came out in September of that year, which was when Wollstonecraft started writing her second *Vindication*. It is plausible, therefore, that she wrote it as a reply to Talleyrand, finishing it quickly so that she could cash in on its currency. This would explain why she chose to dedicate the book to him, and also why her book as it stands focuses mostly on the education of women, rather then legal rights, which, she tells us, she reserves for the second volume. That volume was never written, but *A Vindication of the Rights of Woman* as we know it is concerned with rights at least in this sense: women have a right to be educated, but also, in order to enjoy any other rights, they need to be educated. Thus, I believe, it was not mere opportunism that led Wollstonecraft to dedicate the book to Talleyrand, but a strong sense that he was the right person to whom to address it.

Wollstonecraft informs Talleyrand that her work is a response to his own pamphlet on post-Revolution educational reform. Talleyrand had been put in charge of coming up with a more republican system of education, which he did, but excluding girls. Or at least, girls were to receive an education, but one that would concentrate on the acquisition of homemakers' skills, and that would be conducted separately from the education of boys. Here, Talleyrand followed Rousseau in thinking that women's nature was different from men's, and that this meant they ought to be educated both differently and separately.[4]

Wollstonecraft also tells Talleyrand that her aim is to persuade him and other legislators to include women in the reforms. She appeals to his 'love for the entire human race', which she portrays as the source of his republicanism, and to his strong sense of injustice when one half of the human race is forgotten by the law. Women, she says, are that half now, and even in revolutionary France, unless they have equal access to education, they will effectively be slaves. She wants him to realize that the injustices that plague half of *man*kind leading to the revolution are equivalent to the injustices that still plague half of *human*kind, women, and that the same spirit which led him and others to revolt in order to protect the rights of oppressed men should now rouse them on behalf of oppressed women. She concludes the dedication by stating that reason 'loudly demands JUSTICE for one half of the human race' (68).

More specifically, it is in the Preface that Wollstonecraft announces what she tells us is going to be the main argument of her book, and it concerns education:

> Contending for the rights of woman, my main argument is built on this simple principle, that if she not be prepared by education to become the companion of man, she will stop the progress of knowledge and virtue; for truth must be common to all, or it will be inefficacious with respect to its influence on general practice. And how can woman be expected to co-operate unless she knows why she ought to be virtuous? unless freedom strengthen her reason till she comprehend her duty, and see in what manner it is connected with her real good? If children are to be educated to understand the true principle of patriotism, their mother must be a patriot; and the love of mankind, from which an orderly train of virtues spring, can only be produced by considering the moral and civil interest of mankind; but the education and situation of woman, at present, shuts her out from such investigations.
>
> (66)

In brief, if women are not properly educated, their husbands, children, country and the world at large will suffer. But even here, Wollstonecraft is not merely giving an instrumental argument for educating women – she is not saying that unless we teach her a little morals and politics, a woman will not educate her sons properly and will not be an amusing wife. She is saying that the progress of humanity as a whole will be halted unless it concerns the whole of humanity, be it women or not who are excluded. A human being who does not receive as good an education as the others, but nonetheless has to live alongside them, will inevitably, she says, jeopardize the attempts at improvement of the others. Imagine that there is a fire exit in a university building. It is hidden and only half the occupants of the building are told how to find it and trained to follow the procedures that will see them to safety. In case of a fire, those who know where the exits are will try to go to them in the way they have been taught, maybe hoping that the others will follow. But those who are not in the know will almost certainly panic, run everywhere trying to find a way out, and thereby decrease everybody's chance of getting out safely. This is what Wollstonecraft means when she says that truth must be common to all to be at all useful.

There is an obvious objection to Wollstonecraft's concerns: why not simply exclude the non-educated from any kind of participation? Why not keep mothers at home, busy with simple tasks such as cooking, cleaning and sewing, send children to be educated by male tutors, and generally not involve women in any pursuit that necessitates the use of reason? Women thus 'kept in their place' would not interfere with the progress of humanity any more than a domestic animal does. But Wollstonecraft anticipates this objection:

> I have repeatedly asserted, and produced what appeared to me irrefragable arguments drawn from matters of fact, to prove my assertion, that women cannot, by force, be confined to domestic concerns; for they will, however ignorant, intermeddle with more weighty affairs, neglecting private duties only to disturb, by cunning tricks, the orderly plans of reason which rise above their comprehension.

(67)

So unless women's brains are altogether excised, and replaced by something that responds to order, they will participate in the pursuits of civilization. They will find a way of exercising their natural instinct to take part in human affairs, political and domestic. And if their participation is to be beneficial rather than harmful, Wollstonecraft argues, they had better be educated.

As well as announcing one of the main arguments, in the Preface Wollstonecraft highlights some of the other recurring themes of the text to come, including, maybe surprisingly, a discussion of modesty and chastity. One cannot be properly patriotic without those virtues, she says. But it is men as well as women who should seek to acquire them. She also mentions men's duties as fathers, emphasizing that women will not be in a position to fulfil their duties as mothers until men fulfil theirs as fathers. Already we see that *A Vindication* is going to be concerned with virtues, and that Wollstonecraft does not believe that men and women should have different virtues. Men too, she says, must be chaste and modest; men too have duties as parents they must fulfil. This contrasts with her statement in the Introduction that we ought not to worry about women becoming 'too courageous'. Whereas she was then protecting men's sense of their own superiority by telling them not to feel threatened by the possibility of women competing with them in their field, in the Preface she is not afraid to tell men outright that they need to develop virtues that have traditionally been seen as feminine.

A VINDICATION AS A TREATISE ON EDUCATION

The project of reforming public education of which Talleyrand was in charge was not just a post-Revolutionary project. Since 1760, the French state had been actively engaged in promoting universal primary education. Talleyrand was merely asked to formalize a project that had been put on hold during the Revolution and make sure it fell in with the new ideals. What the revolution brought to the old project was a concern for 'democratization' and 'politicization'. On one hand, universal education was to bring about a more egalitarian society in virtue of children from all backgrounds being educated together. The rich and the poor would get to know each other as equals, and this would consolidate the overall republican spirit. On the other hand, schools were to become a sort of training ground for citizenship and patriotism, and republican ideals would be taught from the youngest age so as to produce good citizens who would perpetuate these ideals (Palmer 1985: 61).

Interestingly, Wollstonecraft seems to agree with Talleyrand on both these points. She does, however, apply them to gender relations as well as to class relations. It is crucial, she argues, that boys and girls should be educated together so as to enable them to learn to live together, to know and respect each other, and not regard the other sex as strange, dangerous, inferior or superior. Familiarity, she believes, breeds respect rather than contempt. Also, as she says in the Preface, education is the way to ensure not only that women become good republican citizens, but that if they possess a good and solid grasp of the republican virtues, they will be able to pass them on to their children, thereby ensuring that republican education starts well, and early.

Dedicating her work to Talleyrand reflected the fact that her *Vindication* truly was a book about reforming the education of women with a view to improving their social and political standing. In fact, Talleyrand was not the first educationalist to whom she intended to dedicate her book. There is some evidence that she was first intending to dedicate *A Vindication* to Catherine Macaulay, a historian and philosopher whose *Letters on Education* she greatly admired. The two had exchanged letters after the publication of the second edition of the *Rights of Men*. The first edition had appeared anonymously, and Wollstonecraft wanted both to express her admiration for Macaulay's work and let her know that the first published response to Burke had been written by a woman. Macaulay returned the compliment and sent her a copy of her own response to Burke, fresh off the press. Macaulay died before the *Rights of Woman* was completed, but it is clear from some of Wollstonecraft's remarks that the work was intended in part as homage to her:[5] 'When I first thought of writing these strictures I anticipated Mrs Macaulay's approbation' (180).

Throughout this book, I will support the claim that *A Vindication of the Rights of Woman* is first and foremost a treatise on education, on women's rights to be educated, and on the need for them to be educated if they are to claim rights for themselves. It was therefore no accident that she dedicated the book to Talleyrand, but a judicious move, advertising her ideas to somebody who was in a position to act on them. In the remainder of this section I offer some detail on the state of education writing at the time of the publication of *A Vindication*, and Wollstonecraft's own writings on this subject prior to this text.

Treatises and manuals on education were extremely common at the time when Wollstonecraft was writing, and juvenilia or children's literature was becoming more popular, at least in part due to the efforts of Johnson (Wollstonecraft's publisher). As Macaulay herself said in her *Letters on Education*, recent 'discoveries' about the workings of the human mind, such as Locke's claims on the power of association of ideas, opened up a whole new field for thinking about education. Two very influential texts had radically changed the way the public conceived of education, in particular, early childhood education: Rousseau's *Emile, or On Education* (1762); and Locke's *Some Thoughts Concerning Education* (1693). Before the publication of these texts, education was not, to say the least, child-centred, in that it did not take as its starting point any well thought-out assumptions about the nature of the child's mind, or about its development. Locke famously argued that a child's mind was as a blank slate, and that early experiences were crucial in the shaping of a child's character. Rousseau argued that a child was by nature good, and that education would either spoil or preserve that goodness. It was therefore the responsibility of parents to see that their children became virtuous adults and good citizens.

Both Locke and Rousseau believed that children's characters developed in particular ways, and that educational practices had to be suited to the various stages of childhood development. Both also strongly believed that early childhood and infancy were crucial stages in that process. On both Locke's and Rousseau's views, it would therefore be a bad idea to send a baby off to a nurse – that would mean missing out on crucial formative years. Yet this was common practice in the eighteenth century. Babies born to rich parents were sent off to live on a farm until they no longer needed to be breastfed, and usually until they could walk and talk.

Wollstonecraft, like Locke and Rousseau, strongly believed that this meant parents missed out on the formative years of their children, and on the opportunity to train their characters. They also noted that nurses could possess unhealthy habits, or carry diseases that would affect the child they were wet-nursing. Hence Rousseau, Locke and Wollstonecraft recommend that mothers keep their babies and ensure they are healthy enough to feed them.

This fresh interest in theories of education prompted writers everywhere to contribute manuals, readers, storybooks, all in some way influenced by what the new theories had to say on early education. Wollstonecraft herself, before she wrote *A Vindication*, had published a manual, *Thoughts on the Education of Daughters* (1787), a book of educational stories, *Original Stories from Real Life* (1788), and an anthology of educational readings for girls, *A Female Reader* (1789).[6]

Wollstonecraft's first published work in 1787, *Thoughts on the Education of Daughters*, reflects her interest in theories of education and prepares the ground for what she argues in *A Vindication of the Rights of Woman*. It is a short tract that emphasizes the importance of early training (following Locke's theory of association of ideas), of mothers breastfeeding their own infants (following Rousseau), some remarks on the difficulties of finding good nurses (a common enough complaint), and towards the end, a description of the plight of educated women who cannot find worthwhile employment outside marriage or demeaning professions such as being a companion, a governess or a schoolmistress, and also an argument against early marriage, as it prevents women from experiencing the world. The work is very disparate and not terribly original, if not for the remarks on the scarcity of employment for educated females. By the time Wollstonecraft wrote it, she had experienced the whole gamut of professions for middle-class women, having worked as a companion, a governess for an aristocratic family, and a schoolmistress in her own schools in Islington and Newington Green. So not only was she familiar with the life of the poor spinster, the name given to women who would not marry, she may well also have considered herself an authority on the education of girls and felt that she had some worthwhile thoughts to share.

Her second published work and first novel, *Mary*, was written in 1788 as a homage to Rousseau's *Emile*, a novel-like treatise on education in which a tutor follows his student, Emile, from his infancy to his married life. *Mary* is a semi-autobiographical work that told the story of the heroine's growth and education. There are interesting differences between Mary and Emile. Mary the heroine (and Mary the writer) are self-taught – they did not benefit from an expensive and free-thinking tutor, but had to scavenge in friends' libraries for knowledge. Also, Mary has little in common with Rousseau's heroine Sophia, and maybe more in common with his hero Emile. This is significant, as one of Rousseau's main points is that men and women were essentially different, and should be educated each according to their nature. Right from the beginning of her career as a writer, Wollstonecraft disagrees and feels that women need to be educated in the same way as men.[7]

Her third work, written in the same year, is less polemical, at least as far as Wollstonecraft's views on the education of women are concerned. Her *Original Stories from Real Life* are simply a collection of highly moral tales told to two young girls by their slightly irritating governess.

One year later, she published *A Female Reader*, a collection of old and contemporary writings suitable for young women. The Preface of that work reflects her commitment to reforming female education, and in particular her desire to adapt some Dissenters' beliefs, such as the importance of learning to read aloud well. This was in part a reaction against prevalent methods of education, which included children learning by heart texts they did not understand. In reading aloud well, one has to modulate one's emotions to the text, so one has to understand what the author is saying at an intellectual and emotional level. Wollstonecraft often points out that prevalent methods such as 'learning by rote' do not lead to intellectual improvement, and suggests changes that would encourage women to 'learn to think' and not to repeat. She is also innovative as an editor as she orders the texts according to themes, arranging them so that they may be compared in such a way as to encourage progress in taste and under-standing. But the choice of texts itself is maybe less innovative.

Most of the writers she explicitly rejects in Chapter Five of *A Vindication*, three years later, are present in the *Reader*, such as Gregory, Barbauld, Chapone and Genlis. Her light challenge to the place of women in society in *Thoughts on the Education of Daughters* is absent here. Women should be educated, but if they are made unhappy by the way they are treated, they must turn to God, not reform. One of Wollstonecraft's contributions to the *Reader* is a set of four prayers through which women may seek 'solace' for experienced hardships. This is very far from her later conviction that solace of any kind was likely to be a consolation prize for injustice received and a distraction from the need to fight that injustice.[8]

REPUBLICANISM AND THE REVOLUTION IN *A VINDICATION*

With her *Vindication of the Rights of Men*, a reply to Burke and a defence of the French Revolution, Wollstonecraft had positioned herself among the radicals as a defender of republicanism. One might expect her second *Vindication* to have put some distance between her political thought and her early concerns on education – that she had 'emancipated' herself as a writer. And yet *A Vindication of the Rights of Woman* is in fact more concerned with the reform of education than it is with establishing political and civil rights. She does not state explicitly anywhere that women should vote, or be granted full citizenship – but she spends a lot of time arguing that strong reforms in education are necessary in order for women to become citizens. She says little of the injustices inherent in property rights and marriage laws, but she defends the view that women's attitudes support, rather than undermine, the injustices of civil life, and that for that to stop they must be educated to think as human beings, rather than simply as wives and daughters. If the second *Vindication* is a republican work, it is not republican in the sense that it explicitly advocates political participation for women.

Nor is it the case that no-one did write about women's political participation. Other republican writers were directly concerned with women's rights: Olympe de Gouges' *Declaration of the Rights of Woman and the Female Citizen* came out the same year as

A Vindication of the Rights of Woman and listed seventeen articles detailing women's rights, followed by a postscript telling women to 'wake up' and claim their freedom. Condorcet's 'On giving women the right of citizenship' had come out a year earlier, and was an attempt to persuade the revolutionary French governing body, the National Assembly, that they should extend their newly acquired rights to women. He argued that women were just as suitable recipients for rights, and just as capable of citizenship, as men. Fifteen years earlier, in America, Abigail Adams wrote to her husband John Adams that 'he should not forget the ladies' as they would not hold themselves bound by a Constitution in which they had no representation.[9]

What these works had in common is that they were concerned with extending the new ideas of liberty and equality to women as well as men: they felt that the love of justice underlying the reforms was only half served if it did not apply to granting women the right to participate. So Condorcet begins his pamphlet by pointing out that enlightened men defending equality for all seem to have 'forgotten' 12 million women. Wollstonecraft agrees. In the Letter to Talleyrand, she quotes the latter's own words back at him: 'that to see one half of the human race excluded by the other from all participation in government, was a political phaenomenon which according to abstract principles it was impossible to explain', and then enjoins him to find a good reason why this does not apply to women.

The above passage does, incidentally, make it clear that, even if she does not make it the focus of her discussion in the present work, Wollstonecraft is fully supportive of women's suffrage and of their participation in government. This may not, otherwise, be obvious. Certainly, Macaulay, to whom Wollstonecraft is in many respects so close, did not include women in her defence of universal suffrage, her reason for their exclusion being that women are too uneducated to become full citizens.[10] Wollstonecraft agrees with her that educating women is a priority, that their contribution to politics, whether through citizenship or meddling, will not be beneficial if they are not educated.

The defenders of female political participation were not in any case more successful than the educational reformers. The French

Revolution did produce a number of feminist thinkers and acti-vists, who met in feminist clubs and salons, of which there were quite a few in Paris. The Girondins, who met in the salon of Madame Roland, were particularly friendly to their cause. Condorcet was one of them. An important member of the Revolution, in 1790 he wrote a plea for the inclusion of women in politics, including giving them full voting rights. The plea was rejected, and three years later, when the Girondins were out of favour, a warrant for his arrest was issued. He died in prison in 1794. The Dutch spy and feminist activist Etta Palm d'Aelders gave several discourses between 1790 and 1792 to various revolutionary clubs, in which she enjoined gentlemen not be just only in half measure. On one occasion, at least, her speech was so well received that the president of the club at which she spoke, in Caen, ordered that a thousand copies of her speech be printed to be distributed to the ladies at their next public meeting. But again, nothing came of her efforts. The revolutionary feminist cause was lost for good in 1793, when Charlotte Corday assassinated Marat, and women were judged unfit for the political life as a result. That year, Olympe de Gouges and Madame Roland were executed, and women's political clubs were banned. Afterwards, the Revolution did not take up the cause of women, and the Declaration of the Rights of Man was amended by the French Republic to include women only after the Second World War.

It is probably because Wollstonecraft does not concern herself directly and overtly with rights that her book received mostly good reviews. She does not scare off the audience, she puts forward some valuable arguments on how best to educate girls, and she offers a thorough review of other educational treatises. And all the time she reminds the reader that men are naturally superior to women, at least as far as physical strength is concerned, a claim that many of her readers would have found comforting. She does not rock the boat. The republican and revolutionary elements of the work were mostly ignored or dismissed as irrelevant overenthusiasm. Probably the readers saw what they expected to see, and they did not expect a woman to write enthusiastically in defence of the French Revolution (Janes 1978).

But Wollstonecraft's *A Vindication of the Rights of Woman* is definitely a republican work. Like the classical republicans, such as
Aristotle and Cicero, Wollstonecraft emphasizes civic virtue and
political participation. But, in common with more recent republican
writers, she also sees liberty as non-domination. Non-domination is
something over and above the concept of negative liberty. Negative
liberty refers to the absence of obstacles. In other words, to be free
in that sense means that one is not interfered with. But that in
itself does not guarantee freedom. A slave who is owned by a
benevolent master who lets her get on with her work and life
without interfering is nonetheless a slave. A woman who is ruled
by a kindly husband is not free. Freedom as non-domination is
something rather more than non-interference. A person is free if
'no one has the capacity to interfere in their affairs on an arbitrary
basis' (Pettit 1999). Arbitrariness here can mean several things –
it can mean that the power someone has over someone else is
unpredictable, or is not constrained by external rules or regulations.
It can mean that it is not a power that was granted for any good
reason – a slave master is not master because he knows better, or
because he has been judged to be more qualified to be in charge
of someone else – he is master simply because he happened to
have the money and the slaves happened to be for sale.

Eighteenth-century republicanism owes much to both classical
republicanism and the concept of non-domination, and it seems fairly
clear that Wollstonecraft[11] was a republican in both those respects.
She frequently refers to the notion of 'hereditary powers' which hold
back both men and women, and confine women to cages. Indeed,
a large part of the argument of *A Vindication* likens the oppression
of women to tyranny. The oppression of women is domination by
an 'arbitrary', 'hereditary' power. She compares the power that
men have over women to that of kings over their subjects – even
though that comparison is complicated by a parallel comparison of
women with despots. But Wollstonecraft is also, as I said earlier,
very insistent that women acquire civic virtues, and emphasizes
the need to help women be 'useful' to the nation by enabling
them to become citizens.

To a certain extent, Wollstonecraft's denunciation of hereditary
power seems to take her thoughts away from other injustices from

which women may suffer. A rich aristocrat, because she is enslaved to looking and acting as is expected of her, is worse off, for Wollstonecraft, than a poor woman who works and looks after her own children. At least the latter is not playing in the hands of a master, but she is in some sense depending on herself and her labour to survive. This is not to say that Wollstonecraft had no sympathy for the poor, or for women who had to both earn a living and run a household of numerous children pretty much unaided. But her focus in *A Vindication* is to help women not be dominated by hereditary power. Aristocratic women are too far gone, she seems to think, to be helped. But middle-class women – those who are sufficiently well off that they do not work, but not so confined by 'hereditary power' that they cannot be helped to think for themselves, women who are still expected to give in to the domination of their fathers and husbands – may be helped, and so she concentrates on them.

Wollstonecraft's republicanism is clearly not simply a denunciation of domination. She is also concerned with women developing civic virtues – at the very least so that they are able to pass them on to their children. In the Letter to Talleyrand, she writes that:

> If children are to be educated to understand the true principle of patriotism, their mother must be a patriot; and the love of mankind from which an orderly train of virtues spring, can only be produced by considering the moral and civil interest of mankind; but the education and situation of woman, at present, shuts her out from such investigations.
>
> (66)

Her way of arguing for the desirability of women developing civic virtues is indirect here, as it appeals to their role as mothers in educating future citizens. Note, however, that she does not distinguish between male and female children, but simply states that all children need to learn to be patriotic.

Wollstonecraft also believes – although she does not argue for it in *A Vindication*, but at least states it clearly (228) – that women should participate in politics as equals and that they should be represented. But it is perhaps the fight for freedom as non-domination that spurs her defence of education in *A Vindication*.

Her proposal that women should be educated so as to become useful citizens and teachers of patriotism chimes in very well with Talleyrand's concern for the politicization of education. She, too, wants to educate children in order to enable them to take the fight for equality a step further.

It is no surprise, perhaps, that most writers interested in educational reform were also republicans – Catherine Macaulay, Anna Laetitia Barbauld, Madame de Genlis. There was the influence of Rousseau, himself both a republican and an educationalist, but also that of the Dissenters, Wollstonecraft's friends who rejected the Church of England and as a result could not attend university. These people were generally republicans and at the same time deeply concerned with education, as their faith meant they had to educate themselves. But mostly, it is likely that it is republicanism that led to educational reform rather than the other way round – for those to whom equality mattered, it was soon obvious that the first step would have to be equality in education.

REASON AND THE ENLIGHTENMENT

One cannot talk about the pairing of educational reform and republicanism in the eighteenth century without also mentioning the Enlightenment movement, and in particular Kant. In an article published in 1784, 'An answer to the question what is enlightenment?', Kant claimed that to be enlightened is to be guided by reason, and that those who receive insufficient education are not exposed to reason, they cannot fully develop their rational abilities.

Kant also argued that it was time for all to throw off the shackles of ignorance, to stop being told what to think by the church and the ruling class, and to 'dare to be wise', learn to think, become the expert on what to believe. This, he emphasized, was not a matter for a revolution – the requisite changes could happen only progressively. Prejudices must be overthrown, and habits must change. But this can happen only over time, with sustained effort on the part of those wanting to change and those wanting to help them. A reform in education is particularly suited to such a project. Education is progressive: it transforms an individual over several years, and a people over several generations. Enlightenment is about expanding one's knowledge, teaching oneself to learn without complete reliance on others, building up one's independent thinking skills – all things that a sound education should provide.

Although we do not know that Wollstonecraft had read 'What is enlightenment?', she was almost certainly familiar with Kantian political thought.[12] Kant was not formally studied in England until the early nineteenth century – but what was taught in universities was hardly relevant either to Wollstonecraft or to her radical Dissenter friends, who were not allowed to study there. On the other hand, the *Analytical Review*, the radical journal started by Johnson and Christie in 1788, to which Wollstonecraft was a frequent contributor, was linked with the *Allgemeine Literatur-Zeitung*, a similar journal from Jena, which published many articles on Kantian philosophy. Those who selected the reviews to translate, as well as those who read them, would become familiar with Kantian political philosophy, if nothing else. Wollstonecraft, as a writer for the *Analytical Review* and a member of Johnson's circle, who dined with him and Christie on a regular basis, would have been familiar with Kant's political precepts. It comes as no surprise that her views on the role of education in politics should match very closely those expressed in 'An answer to the question what is enlightenment?' (Micheli 2005).

Wollstonecraft's thought has not previously been linked with Kant's political ideas, but if she was familiar with some of them, then it is much easier to make sense of some of her own thoughts and arguments. In particular, this help us makes sense of her insistence, from the Preface onwards that women's equal rationality makes it the duty of a nation to educate them, and that this is what will lead them to be granted full citizenship.

Here it helps to move ahead a little to Chapter One of *A Vindication*. In that chapter it becomes clear that the crucial premise of Wollstonecraft's argument for a reform in education is that women are equally as rational as men – this is the other, shinier side of the coin that claims that men are naturally superior to women in terms of physical strength. Rationality is what gives us claim to moral agency, and moral agency is what gives us claim to rights. So, in principle, women should have equal rights. But Wollstonecraft also believes that in order for a person to become a moral agent, he or she needs to develop their rational abilities to a point where they are at least capable of improvement. This line of argument follows the principles of the Enlightenment as outlined by Kant in 'An answer to the question what is enlightenment?'.

In the Introduction, Wollstonecraft makes it very clear that she believes women have rational faculties that need to be developed:

> I shall first consider women in the grand light of human creatures, who, in common with men, were placed on this earth to unfold their faculties.
>
> (72)

and of 'human creatures' she says:

> the human species, when improveable reason is allowed to be the dignified distinction which raises men above the brute creation.
>
> (71–72)

Women must therefore be educated, and Wollstonecraft wants to convince her contemporaries that reforms are necessary in order to enable this. She also wants to convince the French to include women in their educational reform. It is clear that part of her reason for wanting this to be the case is that she believes that women are just as rational as men, and thus need and deserve to be educated to develop their abilities to the same extent and in the same way as men. This is an argument that we will encounter again and again in *A Vindication*. It is also an argument that Macaulay put forward in her letters two years before the publication of *A Vindication*. Morality, Macaulay says, in her twenty-first letter, is the same for all rational beings. Reason, a reliable way of achieving moral goodness, is therefore useful to men and women equally (Macaulay 1996/1790: 221).

The belief that women are just as able to reason as men, and therefore would make just as good citizens, is far from shared by all thinkers of the Enlightenment, and certainly not by Rousseau and Kant.[13] One influential philosopher, Condorcet, made a point of arguing publicly that women were in fact as rational as men, and that as such they ought to be granted full citizenship. He argued that if women do not reason as well as men about political topics, it is not because they are not capable of it, but simply because they are not used to it. That they spend time and effort thinking about their appearance is not a sign that they are less reasonable, but simply evidence that this is the only domain in which they have been allowed to exercise their abilities. If they are given equal rights, they will demonstrate that their abilities are in fact equal to men's.[14]

But Wollstonecraft goes further than Condorcet. A childhood spent learning how to be meek and pretty, or charming and manipulative, is not a good way of developing one's reason, she says. In fact, it is pretty much a way of making sure one's reason is deformed. Women who have been brought up as 'girls', rather than as rational beings, not only will not be capable of claiming their rights and acting as responsible citizens, but they will not want to. This is probably one of Wollstonecraft's most important claims: that we must not underestimate the amount of resistance we will encounter from women we are trying to emancipate. Citizenship is not attractive to one who has been raised to be a wife or mother only – hence the need for reforming the education of women.

In the Introduction, she despairs that their neglected education has rendered women's minds 'weak' and 'unhealthy' so that 'they are only anxious to inspire love, when they ought to cherish a nobler ambition, and by their abilities and virtue, exact respect' (71). Circumstances have made women unable to take up the rights they would be handed if Condorcet had his way. A reform of education must, according to Wollstonecraft, precede any attempt at giving women political rights.

In this, Wollstonecraft is again in agreement with Kant, who believes that throwing off the shackles of immaturity may seem so difficult and dangerous that very few will want to do it, and that those who do will have been so used to constraints that their free intellect will not mature quickly or easily:

> Thus, it is difficult for any individual man to work himself out of the immaturity that has all but become his nature. He has even become fond of this state and for the time being is actually incapable of using his own understanding, for no one has ever allowed him to attempt it. Rules and formulas, those mechanical aids to the rational use, or

rather misuse, of his natural gifts, are the shackles of a permanent immaturity. Whoever threw them off would still make only an uncertain leap over the smallest ditch, since he is unaccustomed to this kind of free movement. Consequently, only a few have succeeded, by cultivating their own minds, in freeing themselves from immaturity and pursuing a secure course.

This attitude, this belief that to become fully in charge of one's rational abilities is difficult if one has lived in shackles for a long time, explains Wollstonecraft's ambivalence when she states her mission. If Wollstonecraft can convince her readers that women are just as rational as men, then it does seem as though it would be hard not to accept the conclusion that women should receive the same education as men – at least insofar as the development of their rational abilities is concerned. However, Wollstonecraft does not feel she can persuade her readers of this very easily, as, unlike Condorcet, she does not believe that women's rational abilities are easily detectable. The very first paragraph of the introduction to *A Vindication of the Rights of Woman* points to this difficulty: 'I have sighed,' she writes 'when obliged to confess, that either nature has made a great difference between man and man, or that the civilization which has hitherto taken place in the world has been very partial.' And although she claims to have a 'profound conviction that the neglected education of my fellow-creatures is the grand source of the misery I deplore', she is obliged to note that the minds of women, in particular, 'are not in a healthy state' (71).

CONCLUSION

In her Introduction, Wollstonecraft tells us that a large part of what motivated her to write *A Vindication* was her observation of the unhealthy state of women's minds, and her perception that this could be remedied only through educational reforms. This means that she will have a hard job demonstrating that in fact women are as rational as men, and that it is possible to educate them in such a way that they can become citizens to the same extent as men, and that they will no longer need to be ruled over by husbands and fathers. It also means that she will have to give an account of how her contemporaries turned out to prefer their condition of near slavery, and how a poor education could take away a desire for freedom and independence. These are all views she defends in the rest of the book, and that we will review in the following chapters.

3

BRUTES OR RATIONAL BEINGS?

Although in the letter to Talleyrand, Wollstonecraft states that her main argument is that women should be educated to be companions of men as otherwise they will stop the progress of humanity, the argument that she defends throughout the book is somewhat different. As we saw in Chapter Two, in order for the argument she states to Talleyrand to hold any water, it has to be the case that women are rational, and that educating them will have the effect of making them useful participants in progress. That women are rational and therefore should be educated was also, we said, Macaulay's argument for equality in education. In this chapter, we explore claims of women's rationality in Wollstonecraft's argument.

UN-GENDERED REASON

In her Chapter One, Wollstonecraft suggests we go back to first principles in order to begin the discussion of women's place in society. She lists them as follows:

> In what does man's pre-eminence over the brute creation consist? The answer is as clear as that a half is less than the whole; in Reason.

> What acquirement exalts one being over another? Virtue; we spontaneously reply.
>
> For what purpose were the passions implanted? That man by struggling with them might attain a degree of knowledge denied to the brutes; whispers Experience.
>
> Consequently the perfection of our nature and capability of happiness, must be estimated by the degree of reason, virtues, and knowledge, that distinguish the individual, and direct the laws which bind society: and that from the exercise of reason, knowledge and virtue naturally flow, is equally undeniable, if mankind be viewed collectively.
>
> (Wollstonecraft 1999/1792: 76).

Let us take these points one by one and try to elucidate them. First, reason is what makes us superior to animals. That is, it makes us distinctly human. This is a point that has been made many times before, starting famously with Aristotle, who argued that although bees had some sort of social organization, they did not have speech or reason, and as such were fundamentally different from human beings. Here is Aristotle's text. 'Logos' here is translated as speech. It does, however, also mean reason. Note how, like Wollstonecraft he immediately links reason to virtue.

> That man is much more a political animal than any kind of bee or any herd animal is clear. For, as we assert, nature does nothing in vain, and man alone among the animals has speech. ... [S]peech serves to reveal the advantageous and the harmful and hence also the just and unjust. For it is peculiar to man as compared to the other animals that he alone has a perception of good and bad and just and unjust and other things of this sort; and partnership in these things is what makes a household and a city.
>
> (McKeon 1941: 1253a8)

Aristotle tells us that reason 'reveals' virtue. Wollstonecraft tells us that it produces it, ('that from the exercise of reason, knowledge and virtue naturally flow') and that, in turn, virtue makes it possible for us to achieve happiness (our 'capability of happiness, must be estimated by the degree of reason, virtues and knowledge'). The latter point is perhaps more reminiscent of Plato than

Aristotle – as Plato famously insisted on the equation of reason, virtue and happiness – but, as we will see in Chapter Four, Wollstonecraft's belief that it is human nature to achieve happiness through virtue and reason is also very much in tune with Aristotelian ideas of the perfectibility of human nature.

The second point Wollstonecraft makes in the above passage is that virtue is that whereby we measure the worth of a human being, compared with others. She means that if reason makes human beings superior to animals, what make us superior or inferior to each other is something slightly different: virtue. In other words, simply being more intelligent does not make you more valuable than another human being. We all have reason – that is the mark of humanity. It is, then, what you do with reason, how you work on it and let it shape your character, that makes you better or worse than another person. This also has religious connotations: what makes a human being valuable is how well they follow the prescriptions of the Bible, how likely they are to find their way to heaven after they die. Merely being intelligent has very little value when it comes to Christianity. It seems likely that the Christian hell would be populated with some very clever men and women who did not strive to become virtuous.[1]

The third point concerns the passions – the emotions – and states that they are an aid to knowledge. This point is rather puzzling, and I propose we come back to it later in this section, once we have filled out the other two points a bit more. It also seems to be rather un-Aristotelian: Aristotle believed that having the right kind of emotions was a crucial part of virtues. But in Chapter Four, I will argue that Wollstonecraft's target here is not so much the emotions in general – like Aristotle, she believes they are important – but a certain kind of emotions, which she often refers to as sensibility, and which are encouraged to grow, especially in young women, at the expense of reason.

Perhaps with the exception of the latter, the principles listed in the passage on page 76 are crucial to our understanding of the argument running through the text. Yet they do not appear to be clearly explained anywhere in the book. This is at least in part because they are based on ideas and principles that would have been familiar to Wollstonecraft's contemporaries. One difficulty in reading eighteenth-century English authors in political philosophy is that we are no longer familiar with many of the texts that would have formed their intellectual background – no-one reads Price or Macaulay, and very few read Smith or Paine. So we need to set the context a little – but once that is done, it will become clearer what Wollstonecraft meant. Her ideas, if not their expression, have not aged.

Let us begin with the idea that virtue is to be achieved through reason, which was very popular among Wollstonecraft's contemporaries. It is clearly in keeping with the philosophy of the Enlightenment – Paine called the Enlightenment 'the Age of Reason'. But it is also a dissenting Christian principle. Richard Price, Wollstonecraft's mentor and teacher, in his *Review of the Principal Questions in Morals* (Price 1994/1787), insists that morality must be derived solely from reason, rather than from God or human emotions. This is because morality must be, according to Price, both necessary and immutable. It cannot be derived from the emotions because these are not immutable, but rather changeable, so no single, lasting morality could be deduced from them.

Price also does not believe morality can simply be derived from God – that would make it reliant on divine choice and therefore less than necessary. It must therefore be made to depend on something that apprehends the truth, an infallible way of ascertaining what is immutable and necessary – and that is reason. A contemporary of his, Catharine Macaulay, shares Price's belief. The twenty-first of her *Letters on Education* is entitled 'Morals must be taught on immutable principles.' In that letter she states that there must be 'one rule of right for the conduct of all rational beings' (Macaulay 1996/1790: 201).

The grounding of morality on reason, the demand that we should regard all human beings, whether male or female, as first and foremost rational beings, is problematic from the point of view of contemporary feminist thought. On some readings, feminist philosopher Carol Gilligan challenged the idea that rationality was the universal ideal that philosophers had made it out to be (Gilligan 1982).[2] She claimed that women's way of thinking about morality was less focused on rational abstractions and more on caring for individuals. Other feminist philosophers have rejected reason as an ideal as 'phalogocentric' − a typically male focus that has come to be accepted as universal.[3] To defend female values, and female rights, they say, we should walk away from this mostly male way of understanding motivations and concentrate on specifically female ways of understanding the world in which reason may not play as big a role. Wollstonecraft is not regarded as a major feminist thinker by those feminists, but rather as an ambiguous figure who is in part responsible for maintaining the *status quo*.[4]

One of the main arguments for not grounding (female) morality in reason is that this is a way of casting aside the emotions, of saying that moral reasoning should not take into account our caring instincts. Reading through page 76 and Wollstonecraft's apparent denigration of the emotions, we may feel inclined to agree with her critiques. Wollstonecraft wants women to think like men, and not very nice men at that. She wants us to think through our moral decisions following the models of games such as the prisoner's dilemma, not taking into account our educated emotional responses to a situation.

This is wrong, however, if, as I will argue, Wollstonecraft's take on all this is Aristotelian. Emotional responses, and hence the education of the emotions, is important as far as Wollstonecraft is concerned − not just for women, but for men. In other words, she does believe that there is just one morality, for men and for women. She does believe that reason is crucial to morality. But she also believes that both men and women need to appeal to their emotions in order to be virtuous, and that for this to be possible, their emotions need to be educated. I will revisit these feminist objections to Wollstonecraft in Chapter Six.

Wollstonecraft's own argument for the claim that there can be only one path to virtue, and that the path can only be reason, is in great part religious. If virtue is what God demands of us, and if he created us for the purpose of pursuing virtue, then there is probably no room for bargaining or excuse-making, but we must all aim for the same perfection. In particular, because God has not specified that virtue should be gendered, then it cannot be so. Men and women must aim at the same perfection and not one that depends on their sex. At the same time, Wollstonecraft talks of the perfectibility of human nature and believes that reason is the tool that has been given us by God in order to tend to that perfectibility. So there is one way that it is better for us all to be: virtue, and one means whereby we might become this way: reason.

One aspect of the line of argument that claims reason is the only way to virtue is that if women are also to be virtuous, then they need to be reasonable. This is the line that both Wollstonecraft and Macaulay are pushing. Everyone wants women to be virtuous – so they can be, at the very least, good mothers and good wives – and if the only way to become virtuous is to apply one's reason, then women's reason should be developed – women should be educated. So the key is to argue convincingly that women are rational, and that they are rational in the same way as men. The view that women were not rational did, after all, have a non-negligible amount of philosophical currency. Aristotle believed that women had no soul, that they were capable of practical deliberation but simply were not equipped for philosophical reflection. Rousseau, who had written much that was admirable on the reform of education, was persuaded, and argued at length that women could not engage in abstract thought.

Wollstonecraft's response to these detractors is to say, very simply, that reason is not gendered. Instead, it is a divine attribute modelled not after man, but after the Supreme Being, God, who is neither male nor female. The argument depends fairly heavily on Wollstonecraft's religious beliefs. If God created human beings with a soul, so that they could perfect themselves and become immortal, then God is unlikely to have created half of them incapable of improvement. To withhold reasoning abilities from women would be to undermine the success of the entire project of human perfection. Had we thought that God had chosen so irrationally, we would then have good reasons to opt for atheism:

> every being may become virtuous by the exercise of its own reason; for if but one being was created with vicious inclinations, that is positively bad, what can save us from atheism? Or if we worship a god, is not that god a devil?

(86)

An immortal soul, Wollstonecraft argues, cannot be gendered. A soul is what helps us towards perfection, through reason and according to the divine model. Giving souls a gender will result only in making half of humanity incapable of perfecting themselves, and so unworthy of immortality. Or it will force humanity to seek perfection according to one of two models. But if perfection is to be like God, then there can be only one model. In other words, if God requires women to be good, then God must have given reason to women in the same proportion as to men. And if God created humanity for the purpose of its own improvement, then God must have given all human beings equal means of making this so.

Could this argument be rewritten independently of theistic assumptions, or does it depend on them? Possibly not: if it is not for some higher purpose that human beings need reason, then it is just as likely that they should have it in different degrees as that they should be equal, and it is not beyond the realm of possibility that one half of humanity should be significantly less capable of exercising their reason than the other, by birth – although following the laws of probability it is unlikely that it could be so.

But it does not follow from this that it is probable that women are that less rational half. In fact, there is nothing to suggest that if one half of humanity is significantly less rational than the other, this half has to be gendered, or even if it is, that it must be women who are the less rational. We would need more arguments to convince us that women are less rational by nature. Such arguments would probably have to be based on empirical evidence. Is it the case, as the economist Larry Summers once claimed, that the unequal numbers of men and women in science is a direct result of a slightly unequal distribution of IQ that only shows up at the top? Summers' claims were discredited because the empirical evidence – the distribution of IQ among men and women – contradicted them.

If we and Wollstonecraft cannot prove beyond doubt, without appealing to religion, that women are by nature as rational as men, the onus of proving that they are not rests with those who believe that women are inferior to men. And a central argument in *A Vindication of the Rights of Woman* is to show that any perceived inferiority of the female sex in general can be explained in terms of the education they have received, and, more importantly, that they have failed to receive. She also spends some time, more notably in her Chapter Two, arguing that those very men who seem to believe that women are not rational cannot express their beliefs without falling into a series of contradictions. Not only is the onus on those who believe women are less rational to prove that is so − but it seems they are doomed to failure.

The religious aspect of Wollstonecraft's thought, highlighted in the above arguments, is often ignored or underplayed.[5] This is in part due to her husband Godwin writing in his memoirs that she was, at heart, an atheist. But even if, by the time she got together with Godwin, she was no longer a church-goer, it is very hard to argue that the writer of *A Vindication of the Rights of Woman* does not believe in God.[6] As we saw above, religion plays an important role in Wollstonecraft's defence of the belief that women are rational beings and that reason is un-gendered. As we will see shortly, it plays an even more important role when it comes to justifying morality − when stating that the reason we should be virtuous is that it will lead to happiness, not in this life but after our death. But before we go into this, I just want to note that Wollstonecraft also expresses very strong reservations about religion, and that she is certainly not ready to accept views on women's nature or place in society simply because they are the views of Christianity. This is especially apparent in her Chapter Two, where she tells us outright that the story in *Genesis* 2: 18–22 of woman being created from a rib of man is not to be taken seriously (92), but was made up by men keen to establish their superiority over women. Again, in her Chapter Five, she refers to this passage to say that it is 'derogatory to the character of the supreme being', in other words, that it gives God a bad name (151).

In her Chapter One, Wollstonecraft puts together the 'perfect-ibility of our nature' and our 'capacity of happiness' (76). But it is unclear whether she means that this happiness is something we strive towards during our lifetime, or only in the afterlife. At times, she seems to think the latter: 'Rousseau exerts himself to prove that all *was* right originally: a crowd of authors that all *is* now right: and I that all *will* be right' (79). Taken together with her often-made claim that to make women wise is to prepare them for the after life, it does seem as though that which she would have us strive towards is something we will get after we're dead. But I think that this can only be part of the picture. She also writes that the discovery of the 'wisdom and goodness' of God, which we make by exercising our rational abilities, makes us 'capable of enjoying a more godlike portion of happiness' (79). This is clearly meant to be a kind of happiness experienced while we're alive. True, her idea of earthly happiness is at times a bit grim. In her Chapter Three, she describes a sensible, properly educated woman who marries from affection, but prudently. She looks 'beyond matrimonial felicity' so that when love dies its natural death she still has her husband's respect, and when she is left a widow she assumes 'melancholy resignation', and if her emotions are engaged in loving her children, 'her brightest hopes are beyond the grave, where her imagination often strays'. It might be good to remember that, at the time when she wrote *A Vindication*, Wollstonecraft had been living a life by all accounts difficult and with few rewards, and that her one loving relationship had been platonic and ended up in her friend's untimely death. It could simply be that Wollstonecraft's imagination was seriously limited as far as earthly happiness was concerned. In any case, she does not deny its possibility.

Whatever her views on the possibility of achieving happiness while we're alive, we have some reason to doubt whether, as far as she is concerned, this happiness is going to have anything to do with passions. In Chapter One, when she tells us what the essential nature of human beings consists of, she says something rather puzzling about the passions being an aid to knowledge: 'For what purpose were the passions implanted? That man, by struggling with them might attain a degree of knowledge denied to the brutes; whispers Experience' (76).

This is hardly a positive image of the passions – they are not something to be enjoyed, something to colour life, but something to be struggled with, and because of that, there has to be a point to them. Passion is always, she says, to the detriment of reason: 'Love, the common passion, in which chance and sensation take place of choice and reason, is in some degree, felt by the mass of mankind' (96). It is a 'deceitful good that saps the very foundation of virtue' (97). And although she allows that 'romantic passion is the concomitant of genius', it only lasts if it is unfulfilled and is not, in any case, immortal (98).

But why, if they are such a hindrance to true happiness, mention the passions at all when discussing the superiority of humans to animals? This is almost certainly because Wollstonecraft buys in to Locke's theory that we learn from experience – and passions, even love, are certainly great sources of experience. Having been disappointed in love herself on at least two occasions at the time of writing, Wollstonecraft knows exactly how much that experience has shaped her, and how, in particular, it has made her more spiritual. Her own disappointments, but maybe even more her sister's dramatic experience of postnatal depression, a broken marriage, and the death of her child, have also helped her reflections on the conditions under which women are expected to live their lives. She understands at first hand what a woman has to overcome in order to behave like a sensible being, rather than a limp doll.

What is also relevant to understanding her attitude is that, throughout the book, Wollstonecraft argues that a certain kind of emotional behaviour, often called sensibility, is encouraged in women at the expense of reason. Women are expected to feel rather than think. They are brought up to be highly strung, emotional beings who are incapable of abstract thought and cannot be told serious news for fear they will faint. This kind of 'passion', however, is rarely conducive to knowledge, and this is why Wollstonecraft is so set against it. Sensibility, and more generally Wollstonecraft's attitude to the emotions, is the topic of a section in Chapter Four of this book.

Before concluding this section, I want to take a look at a reaction against Wollstonecraft's arguments discussed in this chapter. In *A Vindication of the Rights of Brutes*, Thomas Taylor parodies the works of Wollstonecraft and Paine by taking their conclusions to two absurd extremes: that there should be rights for animals and rights for children. These extremes were no longer judged so ridiculous as early as the nineteenth century, and certainly they are now part of current political discourse. But were they really deducible from Wollstonecraft's defence of women's rights? It seems not in the case of animals: women are said to deserve to receive the same education as men, and to become citizens *because* they are not animals, but have reason. In order to argue that animals too have rights, Wollstonecraft would have to either revise her view that animals are not reasonable, or find another criterion with which to decide who is deserving of rights. She does not, in any way, encourage cruelty to animals. In fact, some of her images to express her disgust at the degradation of her contemporaries are derived from cruelty to animals. Also, in her 1788 *Original Stories for Children*, the first 'lessons' she dispenses concern the treatment of animals, how one should observe them without disrupting their habitats, and how we should respect the life of each one of 'god's creatures', even snails, and not experience disgust at their sight. But although these beliefs and attitudes could form the basis for some kind of green politics, it does not give grounds for the claim that animals should have rights.

When it comes to children, Wollstonecraft has quite a lot to say, including thoughts on how, in order to help their growth, we should respect their status as reasonable beings. She derides Milton for his demand that women obey without questioning, by saying that this is what she would expect of children. But, she adds, even then she would tell them to obey only until they have developed sufficient reason to form their own judgments, and then she tells them 'you ought to *think*, and rely only on god' (85).

Also, Wollstonecraft's many arguments regarding the education of little girls may well be grounds for a discussion of the rights of children. Certainly, Wollstonecraft does not believe children should vote. But then neither do we when we claim rights for them: simply, we think that children should receive sufficient education and upbringing, formal and informal, so that they too can become citizens who will take part in political decision-making. Current debates about girls' right to go to school in certain countries are exactly about this: making sure that girls acquire sufficient skills so that they can hold their place in society – the place of a rational being, not of a degraded one. So in that sense, what Wollstonecraft has to say about the rights of children is neither absurd nor dated: it is exactly what we still believe.

EITHER FRIENDS OR SLAVES

One way in which Wollstonecraft attacks defenders of the view that women are not rational in the same way as men is to point out some serious inconsistencies in their discourses. In particular, she argues that no-one who really thinks of women as 'brutes', or as beings devoid of rationality, ought to treat them as her contemporaries are treated: complimented and prevented from using their reason except through cunning and deceit. If women are indeed brutes, then they should be treated as such: 'let them patiently bite the bridle, and not mock them with empty praise' (102). Or they should be treated as slaves, as dependents, but not as the objects of love, friendship or admiration.

Certainly, if they are brutes, women, Wollstonecraft says, cannot be expected to be virtuous, as virtue requires the use of reason. It is not that they cannot aspire to superior male virtue, but that morality is altogether out of their reach. This part of her argument depends heavily on her claim that there can only be one reason and one 'rule of right' for all (102). An objector might reply that we do expect brutes to be virtuous, according to their capacities. Dogs are not rational in the way that human beings are, but dog-owners often find them sufficiently rational to attempt to teach them certain rules of behaviour. A dog who infringes a rule is punished and expected to appear ashamed of itself. At the same time, we cannot expect a dog to understand more complex moral situations, or to resist certain animal urges. So, for example, if a dog bites someone because that person moved in such a way that the dog thought it was being attacked, we do not blame the dog – we do not expect it to understand the subtleties of social behaviour. If a dog eats a sausage that has fallen out of a shopping bag into its bowl, again, we do not blame it. When it comes to animals to which we do not attribute any rational powers, we may still have certain expectations: it is possible to train a hamster to do tricks, and the best way to do so is to use a system of rewards and punishments, which may, to an outside observer, look very like moral praise or blame, but could not be more different.

So there are ways in which one could think that women are less rational than men, or even not at all rational, yet still treat them as moral beings to the extent that they are praised and blamed for their behaviour. But Wollstonecraft's point is somewhat more subtle. Should men treat women as friends and companions, should they lavish them with praise, fall in love with them, if they consider them to be no more than dogs? Some people are very fond of their dogs, but they do not share a bed with them, they do not have children with them and then make them responsible for bringing up those children. They do not fight over them and spend great amounts of money, time and energy trying to win them over. Or if they do, we think them fools. It is this inconsistency that Wollstonecraft is bringing to our attention, this strange inability of men to treat women in a way that is consistent with what they claim them to be – non-rational beings.

Another way in which men who refuse to consider women their equals display inconsistency, according to Wollstonecraft, is in their language. 'As a philosopher', she writes, 'I read with indignation the plausible epithets which men use to soften their insults; and, as a moralist, I ask what is meant by such heterogeneous associations, as fair defects, amiable weaknesses, etc.?' (100). The very vocabulary men employ to describe women betrays the incoherence of these descriptions. A 'defect' is not fair, nor a 'weakness' amiable. At this point, Wollstonecraft is taking the high road and disdains to explain. There is a contradiction, and those who pride themselves on being rational should not make such crass mistakes when describing their fellow human beings.

Yet it does seem there is one way of making sense of the contradiction – a way that renders those expressions much worse than simple mistakes of logic. Frances Power Cobbe, writing on the same subject eighty years after the publication of *A Vindication of the Rights of Woman*, gives us the following analogy (Cobbe 1869/ 1995: 54–74). In China, it was said, emperors would sometimes have infants placed in vases shaped according to their fancy, so that they would grow in them and come out misshapen, for the amusement of the emperor. Women, she suggests, are subjected to a similar upbringing, at least as far as their character is concerned: 'She may freely grow, and even swell to abnormal proportions in the region of the heart; but the head has but a small chance of expansion, and the whole is ricketty in the extreme' (60). In other words, to be 'fine by defect' is to be deformed for the purpose of the amusement of men. It is not any kind of a compliment, but a code for acknowledging cruelty and even sadism.

The analogy of distorted bodily growth is certainly not new with Cobbe, and is one that Wollstonecraft uses in her later chapters. That she does not use it in this context is not necessarily significant – one needs to remember that the book was written quickly, and in instalments, and she may not have had the chance to think ahead of all the points she wanted to make and how they would be relevant to earlier parts of her argument. In her Chapter Two, Wollstonecraft is concerned with demonstrating the inconsistency of men's treatment of women, at the same time as slaves and friends, and of the very language they use to describe these companions. Later on, she points out the cruelty behind the inconsistency.

The clearest example of the inconsistency of men's attitude and treatment of women is to be found, Wollstonecraft tells us, in Rousseau's Sophia. Sophia is the wife Rousseau creates for his pupil, Emile, and in Book Five of *Emile* he explains what her education and her character should be like, emphasizing that it should follow her nature. As far as Rousseau is concerned, men and women have very different natures. Women are not suited for abstract or political thought, and so their reason should not be developed. Their nature is to serve man, to amuse or relax him, so they should learn to obey and to please. Insofar as women are intelligent, they are cunning; they know how to employ their charm and beauty to entice men to serve them, so as to compensate for their natural weakness.

And yet this fundamental, indisputable weakness is also, according to Rousseau, women's means of becoming more powerful than men, of obtaining power over men. 'Educate women like men, and the more they resemble our sex, the less power they will have over us' quotes Wollstonecraft. For Rousseau, this would be a great loss. Women's best and strongest influence, he thinks, has to be over men. If they lose that, they lose their capacity for fulfilment. Wollstonecraft does not agree at all, and she responds: 'I do not wish them to have power over men; but over themselves' (133). If a woman is to be a respectable human being, she ought, first and foremost, to have control over her own mind, both by having been trained to use her reason and moderate her emotions, and by being free to make up her own mind as to what she wants or does not want. This double-edged power is both superior to what Rousseau is proposing – what's the point of getting a man to do things if you can't do the things you want yourself? – but it also presupposes it. No-one can really, or effectively, control anyone else if they are not in control of their own mind. Those who have been brought up to be slaves will not turn themselves into subtle masters with ease.

Yet that seems to be exactly what Rousseau advises: that women, who are in many respects the slaves of their husbands and fathers, should attempt to make slaves of men in return. Rousseau instructs Sophia both that her husband is her master, and how she may keep him 'constantly at her feet' (163). This is, Wollstonecraft tells us, symptomatic of a society in which 'the very men who are the slaves of their mistresses [...] tyrannize over their sisters wives and daughters' (90). But the power of these mistresses is illusory, and the men who create that illusion are 'the most dangerous of tyrants, and women have been duped by their lovers, as princes by their ministers, whilst dreaming that they reigned over them'.

In her analysis of Rousseau's *Emile*, in the first section of her Chapter Five, Wollstonecraft gives us what she believes is the gist of Rousseau's argument: 'the strongest should be master in appearance, and be dependent in fact on the weakest; and that not from any frivolous practice of gallantry or vanity of protectorship, but from an invariable law of nature, which, furnishing woman with a greater facility to excite desires than she has given man to satisfy them, makes the latter dependent on the good pleasure of the former, and compels him to endeavour to please in his turn, *in order to obtain her consent that he should be strongest*' (150–51). And the way for women to guarantee that they retain this power, even after they have given in, is to be vague as to whether they gave in willingly or because they were not strong enough to resist. Wollstonecraft footnotes herself at this point to exclaim 'What nonsense!', and we are wont to agree with her. There is nothing sensible in Rousseau's claims, simply a confession of insecurity in love, and a complete inability to realize that women feel exactly the same way. Wollstonecraft, who at the time of writing this was struggling with unreciprocated love, was well aware of this. What may have seemed to some of Rousseau's readers to be a very subtle analysis of the relations between men and women struck her as sheer stupidity.

But we may still object that, after all, some men do love their dogs, or their horses, far more than is warranted by their estimation of their worth. This was especially true in the eighteenth century, when animals were used for hunting and racing and thus did much to boost the prestige of their owners. Jane Austen's novels are full of young men who think far too much of their animals: fops, as we might call them, rich, inconsequential men, who Austen clearly thinks would be improved if they spent half the money and energy they spend on their own amusement in helping others instead. These men are not always fools: they know that a horse is not a rational being, that it should not be as important to them as a fellow human being in difficulty. But they also know that their attachment to a horse shows the rest of the world exactly how powerful they are. They do not need to look down towards the rest of humanity. They are sufficient unto themselves, and it is the rest of the world that needs them. So the excessive and lavish care for the animal is but a show of power, not real affection. Even if there is real affection, it is only a way of showing how few cares they have that they can engage their emotions so frivolously. Much the same thing could be said of how some people treat their cars nowadays – loving an expensive car, spending too much money on it, is first and foremost a way of showing one's power.

The same argument could be made in response to Wollstonecraft's charge of inconsistency among men who treat women like queens and slaves at the same time. Women are to them expensive ornaments, and any emotion they express towards them is merely a show of power, evidence that they are so strong they can indulge in frivolous feelings. But they do not genuinely hold the objects of their affections in any esteem. It is all for show and there is no inconsistency.

This argument would be convincing indeed if being in love was indulged in only by the rich and powerful. As, however, it seems to be a universal condition of human life, it is very unclear how the argument could work. Falling in love can happen whether or not you are rich. It is not a show of power. If the rich and powerful play at pretend love, that says nothing about whether men in general genuinely believe women to be no more than household pets, or beasts of burden. It only speaks of the depravity of their own emotions. But as love is universal, Wollstonecraft has to be right – treating women as if they are not worthy of respect and adoring them at the same time is an inconsistency.

THE SUPERIORITY OF MEN

One way in which Wollstonecraft appears to offset her claims to equal rationality is by granting that men possess superior physical strength. She makes this claim repeatedly, and at least on the two occasions where she says so in her Introduction, it seems designed to appease those readers who would resist claims to equality. In the third paragraph of her Introduction, she writes:

> Yet because I am a woman I would not lead my reader to suppose that I mean violently to agitate the contested question respecting the equality or inferiority of the sex; but as the subject lies in my way, I cannot pass it over without subjecting the main tendency of my reasoning to misconstruction, I shall stop a moment to deliver, in a few words, my opinion. – In the government of the physical world it is observable that the female in point of strength is, in general, inferior to the male. This is the law of nature and it does not appear to be suspended or abrogated in favour of woman. A degree of physical superiority, therefore, cannot be denied.
>
> (72)[7]

It is fairly clear that this passage is meant to pacify, and also to prepare the ground for the more serious claims to equality – intellectual and moral – that Wollstonecraft is making. A male reader will have felt, upon reading this, that Wollstonecraft was not intending to attack the *status quo*: men are still superior, she says, and she will not argue violently. But we can't help but feel that all this is just a ploy to make her cautious readers more open to the views she is defending. Indeed, she follows this passage immediately by explaining that if men are indeed ennobled by their physical superiority, it is wrong of them to attempt to create further inequalities by using their strength to undermine women's intellectual and moral capacities.

Towards the end of the introduction she seeks to reassure again:

> there is little reason to fear that women will acquire too much courage or fortitude; for their apparent inferiority with respect to bodily strength, must render them, in some degree, dependent on men in the various relations of life; but why should it be increased by prejudices that give a sex to virtue, and confound simple truths with sensual reveries?
>
> (75)

Note, again, that the concession is followed immediately by a request that men do not increase their superiority by diminishing women's capacities. But what is also significant about this passage is that men are said to be superior in virtue, rather than simply in body. True, these are virtues that are somewhat related to bodily strength: Wollstonecraft wants to reassure her readers that women will not become 'masculine', that they will not take to wearing trousers, riding like men, or fighting. Also, she might be slightly tongue in cheek: what does it mean to have 'too much' courage? Is it to become foolhardy? To attempt tasks that are beyond one's capacities? Should men acquire too much courage? Put this way, it seems that she is not in fact conceding anything, merely proffering empty reassurances.

Empty reassurances may well be all men are getting from Wollstonecraft, even when she is talking of physical strength. One writer on the topic, Adriana Craciun, noted that on every occasion except the first, when Wollstonecraft talks of men's physical superiority, she qualifies herself (Craciun 2002: 83). So in the Introduction she talks of 'apparent inferiority with respect to bodily strength' (75). In Chapter Two, she raises the question of men's physical superiority again, 'according to the present appearance of things' (101). In Chapter Three, she writes that bodily strength 'seems to give man a natural superiority over woman' (106).

On the whole, it is therefore far from clear that Wollstonecraft does embrace the view that, as far as nature is concerned, men are stronger than women. And indeed, why should she? Women, even then, lived longer than men. Women, not men, were capable of growing a child in their body, bringing it out, and feeding it. She may well have thought that nature had given men and women different strengths. In any case, she is, throughout the book, very clear that bodily strength is something that women need to seek, that they must, for the sake of their general development, try to develop their physical selves, pretty much in the same way that men do. One cannot help but wonder, therefore, whether she does not think that, if women were properly educated, that difference too would dwindle to nothing.

It seems as though Wollstonecraft's comments on bodily strength are meant as a concession, a *quid pro quo* for the purported equality in terms of reason and virtue. Yet in at least one passage, it looks as though the deal is not quite as straightforward as it seems.

> I am aware that this argument would carry me further than it may be supposed I wish to go; but I follow truth, and, still adhering to my first position, I will allow that bodily strength seems to give a man a natural superiority over woman; and this is the only solid basis on which the superiority of the sex can be built. But I still insist, that not only the virtue, but the knowledge of the two sexes should be the same in nature, if not in degree.
>
> (106)

What is puzzling, worrying, in this passage is the final words: 'the same in nature, if not in degree'. Is Wollstonecraft saying that we shouldn't expect women's moral and intellectual achievements to match those of men? Is she saying that although women too have reason, their lack of muscle will somehow hamper them when it comes to using it to become virtuous? She could be saying this – going back to the passage in which she assures her reader that women will not become 'too courageous', we may deduce that for Wollstonecraft, certain virtues necessitate a strong body as well as a strong mind. A person can be determined to face danger for a good cause, but unless that person is crazy, she will not set out to fight something that is so much bigger than her that she would be sure to lose, if there is someone bigger who can do the job. In other words, women will always hide behind men when it comes to fighting dragons or wars.

But in the very passage in which Wollstonecraft tells us women will not become 'too courageous', she also mentions fortitude – emotional courage. In what sense does emotional courage require muscle? Why should women not be as good as, if not better than, men at fortitude? There are two ways in which we can respond to this problem. The first is to dismiss it and say that Wollstonecraft is clearly simply trying to reassure her male readership, but that she does not mean it. The second is to try and understand why she says this, by looking at what else she has to say on the subject of physical strength.

In the opening pages of her Chapter Three, far from telling us that bodily strength is a poor second to intellectual powers, she complains that it has fallen out of fashion:

> Bodily strength, from being the distinction of heroes is now sunk into such unmerited contempt that men, as well as women, seem to think it unnecessary: the latter, as it takes from their feminine graces, and from that lovely weakness the source of their undue power; and the former, because it appears inimical to the character of a gentleman.
>
> (105)

Moving from the fashionable to the great, she continues to say that maybe those who scorn muscles and health do so because they believe that geniuses are weak, that they have 'delicate constitutions'. But this, she argues, is wrong. Geniuses are strong, and this can be proven through the very observations that may lead some to assume they are weak – their reckless treatment of themselves, late nights, drug abuse, etc. If they can do all this and still be healthy enough to write, paint or compose, then they must be strong indeed! The conclusion she draws from this is that health and bodily strength ought to be cultivated by both men and women. The comment on men's superiority is an aside in a discussion that aims at demonstrating that girls should be brought up outdoors, like boys, and that they should be taught to develop their bodies for strength, rather than just for beauty, again like men. So, when Wollstonecraft enjoins us to let women be educated like men, she means not just that they should be taught the same subjects, but that they should be brought up in the same ways, allowed to develop their bodies as well as their minds.

CONCLUSION

Throughout her early chapters, Wollstonecraft makes one point clearly and repeatedly: that men and women should be educated in the same way, mentally and physically. She consistently gives two reasons for this. First, men's and women's capacity for reasoning is the same, and therefore should be developed in the same way. Second, not educating women means endangering the human race as a whole – education is what enables progress, and the uneducated prevent that progress. Beings whose intellectual powers are frustrated will not by any means refrain from using these powers: they will misuse them. Hence we are better off if every member of society is in a position to use their powers well, that is, if they are educated.

In the course of her defence of these points, Wollstonecraft raises several issues that are worth discussing further. First, she suggests that there is a link between physical health and mental abilities. Neither men nor women can develop intellectually or morally if they do not look after their bodies. Hence the first step in the reform of the education of women should be to allow them to play outdoors, and to engage in activities that will make them strong and healthy. The second point follows from the first. Images of women as fragile or delicate beings are but projections of men's desires to keep women frail, so that they will not compete. Wollstonecraft argues that women are not weak by nature, but that their weakness is the direct result of an upbringing that does nothing to develop bodily strength. In general, she shows that the concept of 'femininity' is full of contradictions. It does not refer to the true nature of women, as this, she says, is only rationality, but it refers to the various roles women are expected to fill: mothers, companions, servants or amusing pastimes.

Of the questions that are left unanswered in the first three chapters of *A Vindication*, the most important is probably whether it is possible to argue that women are rational beings without appealing to God. Wollstonecraft seems to think that design and God's beneficence are sufficient arguments – and why should she not? She is, after all, arguing against those who take seriously the story of the creation of Eve from Adam's rib. But it seems that, if we cannot find an independent argument in the text, this should not overly concern us. We do not really need to argue any more that women are just as rational as men; that particular prejudice is simply gone. Were someone to argue that they weren't, then the onus would be on them to produce arguments, and we would certainly have no trouble refuting those. Maybe a more vexed question that Wollstonecraft raises and fails to answer is what exactly the importance of men's superior physical strength is supposed to be. Are men superior physically, and if so, does it give them any prerogative in any respect? If it doesn't, should we just ignore this difference? Wollstonecraft begins to address the question of whether there are differences that matter between men and women, even though they do not affect basic equality in terms of intellect and reason. But she does not delve deeply into the question, and she does not suggest any answers. Some of what she says seems to suggest that she is, somehow, biting the bullet, accepting that men do have some kind of superiority, and that women do have roles that somehow make them subservient. These early chapters suggest that her thoughts on these matters have not yet matured at the time of writing, that she is in the process of dealing with them, and that she regards them as secondary to the main question of moral and intellectual equality.

4

RELATIVE VIRTUES AND MERETRICIOUS SLAVES

WHY THERE CANNOT BE ANY FEMALE (OR MALE) VIRTUES

We saw that the concept of virtue is central to at least one of Wollstonecraft's arguments in *A Vindication*. Women, she said, should be educated in the same way as men because there is only one virtue – one way in which we want men and women to be good. This does not mean that Wollstonecraft does not recognize that people have different talents that should be developed. For example, she is well aware that some people, like herself, have it in them to become writers, and that some don't. She also believes that a good education should encourage the growth of special talents, and often bemoans the fact that she herself had not benefited from an education suitable for her professions of teacher (she did not know French well) or writer (her reading had been mostly self-directed).

However, diversity of character traits and talents is not the same as diversity of moral goodness. This is clearer if we think about it outside the context of gender. Different women have different talents and capacities, which must be nurtured in their youth for them to realize their potential. Of two girls, one may be suited to become part of the medical profession, perhaps because she enjoys studying anatomy, caring for the sick, and so on. The other may one day become an artist, because she loves to paint and has an unusually good eye for colour. After both getting a good basic education, they may choose to pursue different fields of study that will lead them to their chosen careers. And that would be all right. Giving them the means to engage in a profession for which they are suited will benefit both them and the society of which they are a part. But now, imagine that one of the girls had a tendency to dishonesty and the second is physically violent. Should we give them an education that will nurture these particular traits? Should we make the first an investment banker and the second a soldier?[1] No: we would want to encourage the first to become more honest, and teach the second to distinguish between real courage and mere audacity. That is because we value courage and honesty for every human being, regardless of their natural disposition. Whereas we encourage diversity in talents, we do not do so as far as moral traits are concerned.

And yet, for many of Wollstonecraft's contemporaries, and in particular Rousseau, if we compare a boy and a girl rather than two members of the same sex, the opposite is the case – diversity of virtue is to be encouraged. Rousseau believed that the natural traits of men and women are significantly different and should be encouraged to remain so, even to the extent of forming different moral characters. Because Rousseau believed that diversity of natural dispositions varies according to gender, rather than individually, he thought that gender differences should be encouraged from infancy onwards. For him, this entailed that men and women needed to be educated in different ways so as to encourage the growth of different, gender-specific virtues. This aspect of Rousseau's view translated directly into the educational reforms proposed by Talleyrand: distinct programmes for boys and girls. In order to become good women, girls were asked to foster mostly domestic virtues, whereas in order to become good men, boys needed to know Greek.

In order to refute Rousseau and convince us, it is crucial that Wollstonecraft has some philosophical perspective on what she understands virtue to be. She needs to be able to say why it makes no sense for virtues to be relative. If virtue is simply a place-holder for 'morally good', or 'behaving in ways that are acceptable within society', then it is hard to refute Rousseau's view that men and women have different virtues. There is a lurking theological argument: God gave us virtue, so virtue is divine, not male, and therefore men and women have the same virtue. But that does not really suffice to show that being virtuous will in fact mean the same thing for members of both sexes. One might think that God gives us all courage, but courage for a woman lies in housewifely duties, whereas for a man it means fighting and warring. Wisdom for a man may mean philosophy, but for a woman it means knowing where her duty lies, knowing how to attract and keep a husband, etc. So theology will not, despite what Wollstonecraft seems to say in her Chapter Three, really help.

What I want to argue in this chapter is that Wollstonecraft does in fact operate within an ethical system that tells us that what it means to be virtuous is human, not gender relative. And this system is, I believe, Aristotelian. More precisely, I believe that for Wollstonecraft, a virtue is a character trait that is formed through habituation, that having virtues helps us come closer to human perfection, that a virtue cannot be separated from a form of wisdom, and that virtue is a means between two vices of excess and deficiency. In this chapter, I show how what she says in various parts of *A Vindication* strongly indicates that this is the case. So rather than concentrating on one particular chapter, I will be roaming through the entire book. We will be back on track with a more linear reading next chapter – so if you want to find out what Wollstonecraft says in her fourth chapter, move on ahead to my Chapter Five.

Before I analyse the Aristotelian aspects of Wollstonecraft's theory of virtue, I will need to ask whether she had read Aristotle herself. I will do this in the following section, highlighting the various ways in which Wollstonecraft may have been acquainted with Aristotelian ethics. One serious objection that I need to consider is that Aristotle is hardly a role model for a feminist writer. Feminist philosophers rightly tend to object to a lot of what Aristotle had to say about women – their lack of soul, their fundamental inability to take part in the political life, which is, according to him, essential to human flourishing. But until recently, women philosophers were quite happy to read male philosophers who denigrated women; they would take whatever they found to be useful from their discussion of male morality, psychology, etc., and simply apply it to women, or to humanity in general. There wasn't a great deal of choice, and if you wanted to read philosophy, you simply had to grit your teeth and ignore the worst insults to women. To some extent that is still very much the case, but some women have started to speak out against philosophers such as Aristotle because their attitude to women suggests that their thinking in general might be flawed. After all, people have been suspicious of Aristotle because of what he says about slavery – so why not ground one's suspicions on his writings about women? It may be the case, nonetheless, that this type of rejection of a philosopher on feminist grounds is not as anachronistic as first seems. Wollstonecraft greatly moderated her admiration of Rousseau's work after she read what he had to say about Sophie in his *Emile*. She would probably have felt the same about Aristotle had she been familiar with his views on women's souls.

So let us be clear: I am not suggesting that Wollstonecraft was a great admirer of Aristotle. In fact, as I argue below, she probably had read very little Aristotle. But what Aristotle said about virtue does not belong to him alone. It is arguable that the main tenets of his theory come from Plato, who also discussed habituation and perfectibility, and had plenty to say on the psychology of the virtues.[2] But also, Aristotle's thought had been sufficiently disseminated in eighteenth-century England, by the likes of Hutchinson, Shaftesbury and even Hume, that it would have been entirely possible for a thinker such as Wollstonecraft to reconstitute an Aristotelian theory of virtue without having ever read Aristotle.

THE HISTORICAL PLAUSIBILITY OF LOOKING FOR ARISTOTELIAN ARGUMENTS IN WOLLSTONECRAFT'S WORKS

It is, let us say it outright, extremely unlikely that Wollstonecraft would have read Aristotle's *Ethics*. For one thing, it was not translated into English until 1797, five years after the publication of her *Rights of Woman*, and the year of her death.[3] She could conceivably have read it in Greek, or in an early Latin translation, but there is no record of her knowing the classical languages – she was self-taught, for the most part, and would probably have written of her efforts to learn ancient languages as she wrote of her struggles with French. It is also the case that Aristotle was not well regarded in England in the eighteenth century – his association with extreme Catholicism and Scholasticism seemed a good reason not to pay much attention to his writings. The one exception was the *Poetics*, which was both translated and commented on in French in the late seventeenth century, and English at the beginning of the eighteenth century (Poster 2008: 381, 384).[4] But even if she had not read the *Ethics*, it is more than possible that Wollstonecraft would have come across some of his arguments second hand, while reading some of her contemporaries who had benefited from a classical education, in particular Shaftesbury, but also Adam Smith. Gilbert Ryle, in his essay on Jane Austen, argues that Austen's ethics and aesthetics were decidedly Aristotelian as a result of either direct or indirect exposure to Shaftesbury (Ryle 1966: 298–301). Wollstonecraft, living in London and spending much time debating as an equal with classically educated men, would have had even more opportunity to acquaint herself with Aristotelian philosophy. Another possibility would be that she had access to a 1598 translation of the *Politics* from the French, which is attributed to the poet John Donne. Although maybe not very accurate, this translation was at least complete and would have given Wollstonecraft enough Aristotelian ideas for her to engage with.[5]

Some of the ideas in Wollstonecraft's arguments might strike one as more Platonist than Aristotelian, so someone might reasonably ask whether we shouldn't trace her influences to Plato rather than Aristotle. It is also true that many of Aristotle's arguments as regards virtue and education originated in Plato, in particular the *Laws*, in which Plato describes the importance of the process of habituation in the formation of the virtuous character, and the role of the laws in providing the necessary educational background for this.[6] But Plato's works were not translated into English until after the publication of *A Vindication*. All the major arguments regarding habituation, education and the law could, on the other hand, be found in the 1598 translation of the *Politics*, which she might well have read.

SOME STRAIGHTFORWARD ARISTOTELIAN ASPECTS OF WOLLSTONECRAFT'S THEORY: HABITUATION AND THE PERFECTIBILITY OF HUMAN NATURE

In this section, I show that Wollstonecraft's moral theory is heavily dependent on two theses that are central to Aristotelian virtue theory: that virtues are acquired through a process of habituation, and that human nature can be perfected through virtue.

The concept of habituation is central to Wollstonecraft's views on education and character development. Whenever Wollstonecraft discusses the influence of early upbringing on character, she insists that virtues are formed through habituation. The Aristotelian theory of habituation is mostly developed in the *Ethics*, where Aristotle says that 'moral virtue comes about as a result of habit' (*Nicomachean Ethics*, McKeon 1941: 1103a13). By this he means that virtues, although they are built on natural dispositions, are not themselves 'native', but are the result of character training which took place throughout one's life, beginning in infancy, where, following state laws, parents should encourage children to do certain things regarded as good for them again and again, until it becomes habitual behaviour. Once it is a habit, the moral subject is able to relax and contemplate the kind of actions he or she routinely does, and enjoy performing them – that is virtue. 'Good for them' here means what will help them become the kind of citizens that the lawmakers regard as desirable.

Aristotle presents the concept of habituation most thoroughly in the *Ethics*, which Wollstonecraft almost certainly did not read. But it is in the *Politics*, particularly in the last two books, that Aristotle describes the practical applications of the theory of habituation on the laws concerning education. For example, in Book VIII of the *Politics*, Aristotle writes that character education should be determined by the kind of constitution of which children are to become citizens:

> No one will doubt that the legislator should direct his attention above all to the education of youth; for the neglect of education does harm to the constitution. The citizen should be moulded to suit the form of government under which he lives. The character of democracy creates a democracy and the character of oligarchy creates oligarchy; and always the better the character the better the government.
>
> (1337a10–18)

Wollstonecraft's own words to the Marquis de Talleyrand in the Preface of *A Vindication* seem to echo this passage when she says that mothers need to be educated if they are to teach their children republican values. She, too, believes that education is the making of citizens, and that the virtues we inculcate will be the kind that benefit society as a whole. She does not believe, for example, that we should strive to produce exceptional scholars at the expense of a good education for all – this would not promote the kind of democratic society she is rooting for (Wollstonecraft 1999/1792: 246). Also, like Aristotle, she believes that as the state will eventually benefit from a good education, the state should be responsible for promoting it.[7]

This is very close to what Talleyrand himself wrote – and it is the reason why in France the state had begun to rethink education as state-run and universal even before the revolution. But the idea of state-run education was still in its infancy, and certainly British educationalists were not yet in favour of it. Locke's *Thoughts on Education* also presupposes a strong link between virtue and government. But for Locke, the family, not the state, was responsible for promoting virtues, so Wollstonecraft goes one step further when she insists on children going to state-run day schools. The educational philosopher closest to Wollstonecraft in terms of ideology, Catherine Macaulay, argued that although state run education was ideal in principle, in practice it would be too expensive to run, and there would be too great a risk of it being left to the charge of incompetent administrators and bad teachers. Private or home education, she argued, had to be better than taking such risks with our children (Macaulay 1996: 20). Wollstonecraft, by arguing that on the contrary, state education *is* better, and that in fact it is our only hope of producing decent citizens, is being very innovative.

It is true, of course, that Locke and Rousseau were also very influential on Wollstonecraft's thoughts concerning the importance of early education. Both had argued, against common practices, that in order for a child to become a good citizen, habits had to be instilled from birth, and that it was no good sending the child to a nurse until he or she could talk, because by then their character was already, to some extent, formed. Nonetheless, a lot of what Wollstonecraft writes on the topic is more suggestive of Aristotle than either Locke or Rousseau. Her emphasis is on the process of life-long habituation rather than simply its importance in early years. So in Chapter Six of *A Vindication of the Rights of Woman*, she sets out the mechanism of habituation in the early association of ideas, and explains its importance (191). She argues that habituation has 'a great effect on the moral character of mankind', and that the ideas one has formed from habituation 'can seldom be disentangled from reason'. In other words, habituation forms not only our moral character, but also our intellect. In the same chapter, she goes on to discuss habitual slavery, making it clear that habituation can help form bad as well as good character traits. Her aim in this chapter, it seems, is to raise awareness of the power of habituation, so that we may learn to harness it for the good of mankind, as well as avoid its pitfalls.

Her discussion of habituation continues throughout the book. In her Chapter Eight, she both shows how habitual deception, of the kind advised by Dr Gregory[8] to women (he wants them to pretend they are stupid so their husbands will not feel threatened by their intelligence), can lead to the loss of common sense (210). In other words, pretending again and again to be stupid is not without consequences: habitual behaviour can change character for the worse. Conversely, she also believes that it can change behaviour for the better, and later in the same chapter states that one common moral duty is to 'cherish habitual respect for mankind' (217). In Chapter Eleven, she argues that habit and regularity form duty (235–37); and in Chapter Twelve, she bemoans the 'habitual cruelty' that boys are taught at school (258). She thus displays a rich and varied understanding of the concept of habituation, which, even if it is not derived from a reading of Aristotle, certainly makes her thought sympathetic to his in that respect.

Given that both Locke and Rousseau had almost certainly read as much or more Aristotle – as well as Plato – as Wollstonecraft had, and given that what she has to say about the role of habituation in becoming virtuous and, in particular, in becoming a good citizen, also features in Locke's arguments, is it worth pushing the comparison between Wollstonecraft and Aristotle? It is. Habituation is only Aristotelian if it is part of a particular framework – one that looks at human character as perfectible, as growing towards a natural end. Locke's concept of habituation does not do this. As far as he is concerned, a child is not a 'political animal', a being for whom it is natural to follow a certain course of development, and who will be happier if they do, but rather a 'blank slate'. That blank slate can be written on, the character can be moulded in ways that are more or less supportive of liberty. But if it is a given for Locke that liberty is good for us, he does not argue that it is part of human nature. For him, liberty is good in that it enables us to live together in the least harmful way. It follows that, for Locke, human virtues are also dictated by natural law and natural rights, whereas for Aristotle, they follow directly from human nature. That is, for Locke, a virtue is that which will enable human beings to live together as peacefully and fruitfully as possible, whereas for Aristotle, it is first and foremost that which enables a person to flourish according to their essential nature. Because Aristotle believes it is part of our nature to live together with other human beings, the two are easily confused. But the difference remains that flourishing for Aristotle is directly linked to our nature, which happens to be social. For Locke, virtue is tied to our need for survival in a social context.

Wollstonecraft is closer to Aristotle than she is to Locke in this respect. She believes human happiness is directly linked to the virtues, and that these, in turn, depend on our having reason. She makes these links very clear at the beginning of Chapter One, and again in the introduction to Chapter Four, where she says that 'The stamen of immortality [...] is the perfectibility of human reason' (121), and that:

> Reason is, consequentially, the simple power of improvement; or, more properly speaking, of discerning truth. Every individual is in this respect a world in itself. More or less may be conspicuous in one being than another; but the nature of reason must be the same in all, if it be an emanation of divinity, the tie that connects the creature with the Creator; for can that soul be stamped with the heavenly image, that is not perfected by the exercise of its own reason?
>
> (122)[9]

Here, reason is described as the mark of humanity, its essence, its inner capacity for perfecting itself. This picture of humanity and reason has important implications for Wollstonecraft's views on education. To make the best use of one's reason is not to adapt to a particular set of circumstances so as to be successful in dealing with these circumstances. Of course, that may be part of it, but in educating ourselves we should be concerned first and foremost with improving ourselves, using our reason to become what we are capable of being, and not merely stopping when we think we can handle ourselves in the world in which we live. So, in particular, this means that educating women should not be about teaching them to be successful housekeepers, wives and mothers. The imparting of useful skills is simply not what education should be about, according to Wollstonecraft:

> Into this error men have, probably, been led by viewing education in a false light; not considering it as the first step to form a being advancing gradually towards perfection, but only as a preparation for life.
>
> (122)

All these claims are put forward by Wollstonecraft as a preface to the main business of Chapter Four – to show how women have been habituated by poor education into frivolous, thoughtless and sometimes immoral behaviour. So Wollstonecraft's discussion of habituation is preceded, just like Aristotle's, by claims about human perfectibility through reason and education.[10]

WOLLSTONECRAFT ON THE EMOTIONS

One reason we might be reluctant to see Wollstonecraft as an Aristotelian virtue ethicist is because her position on the emotions is fairly ambivalent. She is very set against a certain type of emotional way of being – sensibility. She feels that in eighteenth-century society, especially in France, but to some extent also in England, both men and women are encouraged to pay far too much attention to their feelings, and too little to their reason. People who are so, who place more emphasis on their emotional reactions than their reason, are referred to as persons of sensibility. They typically appreciate poetry, recoil from practicalities and harsh reality, and have to be handled with care. Burke, the writer of the *Reflections on the Revolution in Paris*, the book that sparked both Wollstonecraft's and Paine's works on the rights of men, was known as a man of sensibility, and was not ashamed either of admitting to being moved to tears by the arrest of Marie Antoinette, or of saying that her beauty and aristocratic dignity were more important to him than any social injustices she may have stood for. Wollstonecraft's reaction to such men and women was one of scorn. She felt that such people had better learn to care for things that mattered, and not trivia, and that fresh air and some exercise would soon cure them of their sensibilities.

A famous literary example of what extreme sensibility could lead to is that of Marianne Dashwood in Austen's *Sense and Sensibility*. Marianne is put forward as an amusing and, at the same time, tragic caricature of how sensibilities can harm a person by preventing them from seeing things as they are, and thus avoiding real harms and dangers. She listens to her current feelings in preference to reason, encourages these feelings to develop strength by the repeated application of music and poetry, and as a result ends up with a broken heart and a fever, and very nearly dies. This is bad enough, but for Wollstonecraft, sensibility is even more pernicious than this. A woman with sensibility is not simply a danger to herself and useless to others, but she is a thing to be toyed with by men and manipulated for their own purpose, like a pretty and impulsive but fundamentally stupid pet. She describes this way of seeing women as follows:

> man was made to reason, woman to feel: and that together, flesh and spirit, they make the most perfect whole, by blending reason and sensibility into one character. And what is sensibility? 'Quickness of sensation; quickness of perception; delicacy.' Thus is it defined by Dr Johnson; and the definition gives me no other idea than of the most exquisitely polished instinct. I discern not a trace of the image of God in either sensation or matter. Refined seventy times seven, they are still material; intellect dwells not in there; nor will fire ever make lead gold!
>
> (133)

What sensibility amounts to, then, is the unnatural growth of the emotions independently of reason. Wollstonecraft compares the woman of sensibility with a hot-house flower, which has exotic beauty but no use and no strength. But in fact, rejection of sensibility is not rejection of the emotions. Far from rejecting the emotions, from her very first chapter Wollstonecraft emphasizes that both reason and emotions have a role to play in morality. The role of reason is clear: that we are rational is that which enables us to be moral, and we increase our virtue though our reason. The role of the emotions is less clear. 'For what purpose were the passions implanted? That man by struggling with them might attain a degree of knowledge denied to the brutes; whispers Experience' (75). This is, it must be acknowledged, a rather cryptic statement. Why does knowledge come from the passions rather than reason, and if the passions are instrumental in bringing us knowledge, then why don't the beasts have knowledge also? Isn't reason what distinguishes us from beasts and passions what bring us closer to them?

One way to answer these questions is to say that Wollstonecraft, having reflected on the effect of passions, had concluded that the best thing to do about them was to struggle against them.[11] This fits with her earlier suggestion in *Thoughts on the Education of Daughters* that passions had been implanted in humanity by God for the very purpose of teaching us how to struggle with ourselves. By struggling with our passions, we achieve greater self-knowledge and greater self-control, both of which Wollstonecraft held to be highly valuable. Indeed, to Rousseau's claim that if women are educated they will lose power over men, Wollstonecraft replies tersely that she wishes women to have power only over themselves (133).

When women are described as creatures of 'sensibility' in whom reason is not as powerful or indeed useful as the emotions, they are said to differ from men, who will appeal to reason before the emotions. Wollstonecraft does not approve of this distinction: men and women, she says, will benefit equally from being led by reason. But for her, this does not mean just that reason should be educated in girls as much as it is in boys. She also strongly believes that boys' and girls' emotions should be properly educated. This is born out by her insistence, in the final chapter of the book, that boys and girls alike should be educated in day schools. The point of such an education would be first, to habituate boys and girls to be together, so that they have well regulated emotions towards each other and do not react in extreme ways when they meet after their schooling is over and they are susceptible to irrational love. But also, the point of day schools is that children benefit on one hand from a teacher who is not dependent on their family and the company of peers that only school can offer, and also from the proper emotional upbringing that only a family setting can offer. Wollstonecraft does not believe that the emotions can be well educated either exclusively at home, where children do not engage with their peers and so do not develop confidence and the ability to think for themselves; or in boarding schools, where children do not benefit from parental love and guidance. As we will see in some detail in Chapter Eight of this book, she speaks very disapprovingly of the bad character habits acquired in boarding schools by both girls and boys.

What Wollstonecraft seems to object to, then, is not so much that the emotions should have a role to play in living virtuously, but the pernicious habit of wallowing in one's own emotions to the exclusion of reason, which she sees the person of sensibility as engaging in. On the contrary, Wollstonecraft appears to believe that in order to become virtuous, one must educate one's emotions as well as one's reason. Children must be brought up with the right mixture of parental love and independence; and girls and boys must be exposed to each other throughout their lives so they are used to regarding each other as fellow human beings, people they can relate to and count on to experience life in a very similar way, rather than exotic creatures that simply excite their emotions and desires. Wollstonecraft, no less than Aristotle, believes that to be virtuous is in part to have certain good emotional responses to situations, and that children can be taught to have these emotions.

Having argued convincingly, I hope, that Wollstonecraft's theory of virtue is Aristotelian in that it relies on the concepts of habituation and perfectibility of human nature, and that, far from denigrating the role of the emotions in virtue, she believes that emotions need to be educated, I now want to turn to the specific cases of two virtues she discusses at length: chastity and modesty. In the following two sections I hope to show first that for Wollstonecraft, as for Aristotle, virtue is incompatible with ignorance; and second that a virtue is a mean to which correspond two vices of deficiency and excess.

VIRTUE AS A MEAN: CHASTITY

Maybe the best known feature of Aristotle's virtues is the thought that virtue is a mean between two extremes: the vice of deficiency and the vice of excess. So someone who fails to be courageous may do so in two ways. They may be cowardly (deficiency) or they may be foolhardy (excess). That is, they may be excessively cautious in the face of danger, or excessively careless. Being courageous means being able to judge the exactly right measure of braving danger required in any given situation. It means being able to assess the danger, and to assess one's capacity to fight it and that of others involved. For example, if a child is drowning and I am the only swimmer on the scene, then it would be cowardly not to jump in. If, on the other hand, I jump in when there are lifeguards on the scene and get in their way, I am foolhardy. Thus being courageous depends very much on being able to make a judgement on the relevant particulars of the situation; in other words, it depends on the exercise of reason.

That Wollstonecraft embraces the notion of virtue as a mean is especially clear in her discussion of modesty and chastity. Despite her rejection of conceptions of femininity centred on chastity, Wollstonecraft does truly believe that chastity is a virtue. But rather than accepting what others have said on the topic, and merely claiming a certain very strict etiquette for women, she defines chastity as an Aristotelian virtue – as a mean to which correspond two vices of extreme.

Wollstonecraft's discussion of chastity is somewhat complicated by her linking of chastity and modesty. She seems to believe that the two virtues are interdependent. First, chastity is 'purity of mind' and it is necessary if one is to possess modesty: 'the simplicity of character that leads us to form a just opinion of ourselves' (198). Here, Wollstonecraft seems to tell us that unchaste behaviour somehow pollutes the mind such that it is harder to form a good appreciation of our own worth. She possibly means that a woman who has extra-marital affairs and who is praised by lovers may well have an over-inflated sense of herself. This would be in keeping with her general attitude to unfaithfulness.

The second way in which Wollstonecraft believes chastity and modesty to be related is this: she claims that in order to be truly chaste, one must be modest. This makes sense, perhaps, if we consider that chastity and modesty for women are often linked in this way in religious thought. The modesty that is so praised by Islam, for example, and that results in some women covering their hair and face, and wearing demure clothing, is directly linked to the possibility that they may attract members of the opposite sex and cause them to engage in extra-marital sex. Again, it is clear that when Wollstonecraft condemns French women for their lack of modesty, she refers in part to their more revealing clothes, with very low necklines, which she regards as an indication of their willingness to engage in lewd behaviour.

With these clarifications in mind, let us now turn to the question of whether modesty and chastity in Wollstonecraft are virtues in the Aristotelian sense of having two corresponding vices of extreme and deficiency.

That modesty is a virtue that corresponds to two vices for Wollstonecraft is clear: humility is deficiency, and arrogance or vanity is excess. 'Modesty,' she says, 'is that soberness of mind which teaches a man not to think more highly of himself than he ought to think, and should be distinguished from humility, because humility is a kind of self-abasement' (198). She goes on to establish that modesty is a virtue, and humility and vanity vices, by stating that 'A modest man is steady, and humble man timid, and a vain one presumptuous.' Steadiness, we already know, she regards as a necessary quality of virtue. A virtue cannot simply disappear in adversity. It must manifest itself in all circumstances – even if it is only as a ruin. She illustrates her point by pointing to the modesty of Washington when he took on the command of the army: 'The latter has always been characterized as a modest man; but had he been merely humble, he would probably have shrunk back irresolute, afraid of trusting to himself the direction of an enterprise, on which so much depended' (198). Then, provocative as ever, she concludes: 'Jesus Christ was modest, Moses was humble, and Peter vain' (199).

If chastity is also a virtue, then it must have corresponding vices of excess and deficiency. The vice of deficiency is not hard to find, and Wollstonecraft is very vocal about it: one can be unchaste by failing to resist sensual temptations, giving in to passions, being a libertine. But what of the vice of excess? Can one be too chaste? Wollstonecraft is, perhaps understandably, more vague on this. But she does allude to such a vice, it seems, when she talks of Heloise, the philosopher and lover of Abelard, who retired to a convent because she could not consummate her marriage to the man she loved (he was castrated). 'The victory is mean,' Wollstonecraft says, 'when they merely vanquish sensibility. The real conquest is that over affection not taken by surprise – when, like Heloisa, a woman gives up all the world, deliberately, for love. I do not consider the wisdom or virtue of such a sacrifice, I only said that it was a sacrifice to affection, and not merely to sensibility, though she had her share' (203–4). So Heloise's giving up sex was chaste because she did it for love. But to give up sex altogether just because it is sex, just because one wants to cut oneself from sensuality, is not chaste. That kind of self-denial, Wollstonecraft seems to be telling us, is the vice of excess.

In fact, Wollstonecraft appears to believe that practices that would teach girls abstinence and ignorance of sensuality encourage the opposite vice. Women who are kept away from men, who are denied any insight into their sensuality will, she says, simply turn to each other in an immodest way. Here it may look as if she is simply attacking homosexual practices – she refers to what girls get up to when they sleep in dormitories together, talks about the 'nasty tricks' they learn at school. But this needn't be how we interpret her. It may simply be that what Wollstonecraft is objecting to is unreasoned, undirected sensuality, intimacy without respect, as she says that those women 'have not been taught to respect the human nature of their own sex'. She finds the indiscriminate sexual behaviour that she imagines women thrown together and excluded from the world to engage in objectionable, not because it is homosexual, but because it lacks human dignity.[12] Chastity, as modesty, requires a knowledge and love of humanity, and this is what girls shut up in convents paradoxically lack.

VIRTUE AND WISDOM: BASHFULNESS VERSUS MODESTY

One thing Wollstonecraft makes very clear throughout the book, but in particular in her Chapter Seven, is that it is absurd to expect women to be virtuous in any way while keeping them ignorant. Virtue can only be achieved through reason, and reason must be developed to function at all well. This is exactly what an Aristotelian virtue ethicist would say: virtue is not compatible with ignorance, but must be learnt, not only through habituation, but in a way that makes it possible to reflect on what virtuous behaviour consists of.

For that reason, Aristotle distinguishes virtues from natural dispositions. Natural dispositions are the traits we are born with, or develop at a very young age, and they fall short of virtues in several ways, mainly because they are malleable and unreliable. Someone who is naturally kind may nonetheless treat a person badly because they are prejudiced. Mark Twain's hero Huckleberry Finn has a strong natural sense of justice. But when it comes down to it, he thinks that by not turning in his companion Jim, the runaway slave, he is doing something morally wrong. His natural leanings towards justice stumble on his learned prejudices: a black man is a slave, and a slave is by rights the property of the person who purchased him. Were he able to identify these beliefs as prejudices, he would have no doubt that helping Jim escape was the right thing to do. What he lacks is the ability to reflect on all the relevant aspects of his situation, to question his relevant beliefs. He lacks a certain kind of wisdom.

Of course, good natural dispositions are an asset. Being disposed to be empathetic by nature will be of help when learning the virtue of compassion. But it does not by itself count as a virtue. One can empathize with the suffering of someone without it being virtuous. Someone who has not given a great deal of thought to the matter of suffering may be moved by the spectacle of a hurt kitten, but fail to respond in any way that is commensurate when told of starving children in Africa. This is a failure of judgment concerning the degree of suffering involved. Or one may be moved to help someone because they need it, interpreting their suffering correctly but choosing to help inappropriately, in the wrong way at the wrong time. A person wanting to help a friend in emotional distress may offer them highly addictive drugs that they know will relieve the immediate pain, but without reflecting on the harm they are causing them by potentially turning them into addicts. Again, the choice reflects a lack of wisdom, a failure of reason.

Wollstonecraft makes the very same point, that a positive trait is a virtue only if it is strengthened by reason, when she says that 'modesty is a virtue, not a quality' (199). She illustrates this point vividly by describing the case of prostitutes:

> The shameless behaviour of the prostitutes, who infest the streets of this metropolis, raising the alternate emotions of pity and disgust, may serve to illustrate this remark. They trample on virgin bashfulness with a sort of bravado, and glorying in their shame, become more audaciously lewd than men, however depraved, to whom this sexual quality has not been gratuitously granted, ever appear to be. But these poor ignorant wretches never had any modesty to lose, when they consigned themselves to infamy; for modesty is a virtue, not a quality. No, they

were only bashful, shame-faced innocents; and losing their innocence, their shame-facedness was rudely brushed off; a virtue would have left some vestiges in the mind, had it been sacrificed to passion, to make us respect the grand ruin.

(199)

The point she makes is that virtues must be firm character traits, not fleeting dispositions; they must manifest themselves in difficult as well as in comfortable situations. A similar point was made in the second half of the twentieth century by social psychologists who wanted to question the existence of virtue. They conducted certain experiments designed to show how so-called virtues would take the back seat in certain circumstances. One such experiment was the Good Samaritan experiment (Darley and Batson 1973). Students of a New York seminary were asked to go and teach a class on the topic of the good Samaritan in another building. On their way, an actor was waiting, pretending to be the victim of a mugging in need of their help. The story of the Good Samaritan, on which they had been asked to lecture, was about apparently good people failing to extend help to somebody in just that kind of situation. Yet not all the subjects of the experiment helped. Notably, those who were in the greatest hurry, or who had been told about the lecture at the last minute, tended not to stop. In other words, their dispositions to be helpful were not very reliable, they were not virtues. This experiment probably says more about the scarcity of truly or completely virtuous people than it does about whether or not there is such a thing as virtue. But it is not incompatible with the Aristotelian thesis that character traits must be transformed and strengthened through years of habituation before they are firm enough to be called virtues.

Wollstonecraft recognizes that virtues are unlike natural dispositions in that they are firm, and that they can only become so if they are teamed with wisdom. But her analysis is subtle: she does not claim implausibly that, once acquired, a virtue will always assert itself no matter what. She recognizes that adversity or passion may be strong enough to destroy a virtuous character. But such a character is still to be distinguished from those who were never virtuous. It is a 'grand ruin' and presumably inspires more pity than disgust, as one knows exactly how much was lost.

She carries on to say that:

> To render chastity the virtue from which unsophisticated modesty will naturally follow, the attention should be called away from employments which only exercise the sensibility; and the heart made to beat time to humanity, rather than to throb with love. The woman who has dedicated a considerable portion of her time to pursuits purely intellectual, and whose affections have been exercised by humane plans of usefulness, must have more purity of mind, as a natural consequence, than the ignorant beings whose time and thoughts have been occupied by gay pleasures or schemes to conquer hearts.
>
> (200)

What is wrong with the 'innocence' of the women who become prostitutes, or at least what makes it less than a virtue, is the fact that it is not based on reflection and understanding. It is instinctive and reason has no part in it. But like Aristotle, Wollstonecraft believes that virtues are acquired through both practice and the exercise of reason. In order to be virtuous, one must have attained a certain degree of rationality, and one must have been actively trying to be virtuous, caring for others. She is very clear that the simple-minded and those who do not take part in human activities cannot be virtuous. This also has implications for a more commonly accepted picture of chastity – that of the pure yet uneducated nun, who never leaves her cell, as a paragon of virtue. Wollstonecraft would question the idea that such a woman is in fact saintly – as she believes that God wants us to be rational, not ignorant and stupid. In any case, her idea of virtue has very little to do with what her contemporaries understood by feminine virtues. Her virtue is un-gendered, and depends on reason.

CHASTITY AND MODESTY IN THE TWENTY-FIRST CENTURY: AN ANACHRONISM?

One may wonder whether the emphasis she places on discussing the virtues of modesty and chastity makes Wollstonecraft's writings somewhat irrelevant to modern feminist concerns, and whether that might not be a good reason why Wollstonecraft is so rarely quoted in feminist writings. Of course, Wollstonecraft does not believe, and she makes it very clear that she does not, that chastity and modesty are the most important virtues, or that they are, in any sense, womanly virtues. She spends time discussing them because they are commonly held to be the only virtues a woman should develop. But this is precisely what might make us question the relevance of her writings to today's feminist concerns. The charge is not that Wollstonecraft defends chastity and modesty as important virtues, but that she has to discuss them at all. The discourse, we might feel, has moved on. Nobody expects women to be chaste or modest. These are outdated virtues, and if there is a prejudice that men and women should have different virtues, then it does not concern modesty and chastity.

This is wrong, of course. Concerns of modesty and chastity are still clearly part of what makes it difficult to be a woman in the twenty-first century. For some women, this is perhaps a more pressing concern than it was for Wollstonecraft's contemporaries, those women who cannot be seen without a veil, or leave the house unchaperoned for fear of being raped. The rhetoric is the same: if a woman chooses to display herself in public, she is unchaste, and that makes her less than human, undeserving of the respect that is due to a virtuous person. This is something that happens frequently in some African countries, but also in the suburbs of Paris, where young women feel they must either dress as boys or be veiled in order not to be raped. In those situations, much importance is placed on a woman's reputation. If she somehow manages to acquire a reputation as somebody who does not abstain from sexual intercourse, or who will allow men to regard her as a sexual object, then she is deemed available, that is, deserving of rape and, often, gang rape.[13]

This is not, by any means, something that only Muslim women suffer. Women are still thought of as 'provocative' and somehow deserving of abuse if they do not conform to certain fairly stringent standards of chastity. The most common outcome of a rape court case in the UK is still a verdict of not guilty – fewer than 6 per cent of cases result in conviction. From 1976 until 2003, men could claim a defence of 'honest belief in consent'. In 2003 this was revised somewhat, and men now have to show they took reasonable steps to ascertain consent. But it is not clear what could be regarded as reasonable, and it seems that attitudes still tend to place very little weight on women's utterances in this respect. For instance, during an incident in Yale in October 2010, some fraternity men marched through campus chanting 'No means Yes, and Yes means anal'. It seems, unfortunately, that obtaining consent relies on very little indeed. A woman wearing a short skirt, being out at night alone, drinking too much, wearing a lot of make-up is still, for a lot of people, a woman saying 'yes' while her lips say 'no'. In order to be in a position to emit a convincing 'no', a woman is expected to be chaste: not to be open about her sexuality, not to enjoy herself in an environment frequented by men, and not to do anything to make herself attractive. If she does any of this, there will still be men who believe that she is consenting to intercourse with them.

In both types of case, Wollstonecraft's discussion of chastity is highly relevant. Chastity for women, she would say, should not be a matter of creating a reputation for purity so that one is left alone, it should stem from a genuine desire to engage in sexual relations only when one feels it is the right thing to do. But she would mostly emphasize that those in real need of chastity lessons are men, those very men who assume that the desire they experience when they look at an attractive woman translates into a right to have intercourse with her. Men, she would say, need to learn to control their urges and not see them as more important than the respect they owe to another human being.

Modesty is also a virtue that is still misinterpreted in the very same ways that Wollstonecraft denounces. Women are often expected to underplay their abilities and their ambitions. If they do not, they are characterized as 'brash', 'unfeminine'. In the workplace, women's self-perceptions of their competence are typically lower than those of their male counterparts. This is matched by inequalities in salary and promotions. Women are being held back by what they perceive as modesty, but what Wollstonecraft would term humility, whereas men, more confident, sometimes exhibit pride and reward each other accordingly. A better understanding of what it means to be truly modest – to strike the right balance between humility and pride – may lead to a better chance of closing the professional gender gap.[14] Once again, Wollstonecraft's discussion is highly relevant.

CONCLUSION

It would not be right to assert that Wollstonecraft adopted an Aristotelian virtue ethics, or indeed that she consciously sided with any particular philosophical movement. Although an avid reader, she had not spent years studying at university, or even at home, free from other responsibilities, so she was probably famil-iar with most philosophical literature only second-hand – through reading reviews and accounts in other books, and conversing with her male friends. Yet the extent to which her writings on the virtues match an Aristotelian account is striking. Her discussions of the role of habituation, her constant emphasis on the perfectibility of human nature, her belief that the emotions need to be educated, and her discussion of the virtues of modesty and chastity altogether produce a very Aristotelian picture. That she may not have been familiar with Aristotle is neither here nor there. It may, in some sense, be even more interesting if Wollstonecraft turned out to be Aristotelian despite having never read Aristotle. Annette Baier, in her 'What do women want in a moral philosophy' (Baier 1994), argues that women moral philosophers seem to be more inclined towards Aristotelian virtue ethics than say, Utilitarianism or Kantianism. She lists as evidence a number of women philosophers who are indeed that way inclined, including Philippa Foot, Elizabeth Anscombe, Iris Murdoch and many others. She explains this phe-nomenon by suggesting that the kind of moral theorizing that can be done with Aristotelian ethics is best able to reflect two concerns that women have in thinking about morality: the centrality of care, and the difficulty inherent in dealing with particular cases. It strikes me that Baier should have included Wollstonecraft in her list, and shown that the tendency was somewhat more than a late twentieth-century fashion.

5

ABJECT SLAVES AND
CAPRICIOUS TYRANTS

WOMEN WITHOUT VIRTUE

In Chapter Four we looked at the theoretical background against which Wollstonecraft may have operated, and we saw that it was a mixed background – with some influences from Locke and Rousseau – but with strong Aristotelian tendencies. Throughout *A Vindication of the Rights of Woman*, but maybe mostly in Chapter Four, she attempts to derive from these ethical views an understanding of the situation in which her contemporaries find themselves. In particular, she seeks to explain why women can appear at the same time as slaves and tyrants, and why women have not at least tried to fight their oppression. In doing this, Wollstonecraft distinguishes herself from almost any other writer on this topic, and she offers a subtle analysis of a socio-political phenomenon that still concerns us today in the context of global justice.

Wollstonecraft's Chapter Four professes to be a study of the state of degradation of women. But what it does mostly focus on is those aspects of women's degradation that make them less likely to want to right their position. Women, she argues, when they have been degraded in certain ways, lose some of their humanity, they become stunted. Wollstonecraft's project here is to show how this degradation occurs, that it is in fact degradation, and not the natural state for women to be in, and how it may, eventually, be overcome. But because she is describing the long-term effects of women being treated as fundamentally different from, and toys for, men, she can sometimes be harsh in her descriptions. The women she is talking about are triflers, they pursue goods of very little worth and ignore those that are genuinely valuable. In other words, men have succeeded in rendering them less than human.

Chapter Four of *A Vindication* begins with the report of an observation that, if the greater part of mankind is enslaved, one way or another, and they are not doing anything about it, then they must find some compensation in their condition.

> Men, they further observe, submit every where to oppression, when they have only to lift up their heads to throw off the yoke; yet, instead of asserting their birthright, they quietly lick the dust, and say, let us eat and drink, for tomorrow we die.
>
> (121)

This, Wollstonecraft tells us, is also true for women who 'are degraded by the same propensity to enjoy the present moment; and, at last, despise the freedom which they have not sufficient virtue to struggle to attain' (121). Whereas Wollstonecraft certainly does not think that women are to blame for their own degradation, she believes that the lack of virtue which is part of that degradation is what prevents them from fighting back. By making them their 'slaves', men take away from women the firmness of character traits that they would need in order to free themselves, or even in order to value their freedom. This same thought is expanded a few pages later:

> Confined then in cages like the feathered race, they have nothing to do but plume themselves, and stalk with mock majesty from perch to perch. It is true that they are provided with food and raiment, for which they neither toil nor spin; but health, liberty, and virtue, are given

in exchange. But, where, amongst mankind, has been found sufficient strength of mind to enable a being to resign these adventitious prerogatives; one who, rising with the calm dignity of reason above opinion, dared to be proud of the privileges inherent in man? And it is vain to expect it whilst hereditary power chokes the affections and nips reason in the bud.

(125)

So women are enslaved, but receive enough attention that they prefer to remain that way, while at the same time their status means they cannot value the freedom that is rightly theirs, but prefer to remain as they are. In the following sections I address the paradox of why women, according to Wollstonecraft, prefer to be enslaved.

SENSIBILITY: A SICKNESS OF THE TIMES

The whole of A *Vindication*, and particularly Chapter Four, is ripe with references to women's condition as slavery. In this section I focus on the contention that women, at least Wollstonecraft's contemporaries, were indeed enslaved, and try to figure out what that might mean.

When Wollstonecraft writes about slavery, her points of reference would be first, the condition of peasants in pre-Revolutionary, feudal France, and second, African slaves in America. She also refers a few times to slavery in Ancient Greece. If she had read Aristotle's *Politics*, she would be familiar with his extraordinarily poor argument for the conclusion that there is such a thing as natural slavery, and that those who are strong in body are by nature suited to be slaves (*Politics*, McKeon 1941: 1253b–1256a). Her own emphasis on the importance of physical strength, for both men and women (discussed in my Chapter Three), might then be seen as a direct disagreement with Aristotle's theory.

England, unlike France, was not feudal in the eighteenth century. As a member of the middle classes, Wollstonecraft did not owe anything to anyone, and was therefore as far from the condition of an 'enslaved' peasant as it is possible to be. As to the life conditions of African slaves, she would have been aware that they were unbearable – anti-slavery movements were growing in Britain at the time she was writing, and the Dissenters, including Price, were involved in calls for the abolition of the slave trade. Many pamphlets were written for the purpose of gaining support for abolitionism. It was widely known that families were separated by force and that many were killed during capture and transportation. Former slaves such as Olaudah Equiano, who was touring Britain shortly before Wollstonecraft started working on *A Vindication*, raised awareness of the horrors of life on the plantation. That she possessed this background knowledge, and that it was widely disseminated and the subject of much political debate, probably meant that Wollstonecraft would not have spoken of slavery lightly.[1]

It may seem as though the comparison is an exaggeration, and shows either ignorance or, since Wollstonecraft was almost certainly well informed on that topic, disrespect to the African slaves. But we should bear in mind that the conditions of life for women in the eighteenth century could be very bad indeed. Those who had good lives were mostly lucky that their husband or father chose to treat them well. Although British women were not forced to work in the fields, and were not chained or forced to live in shacks, there seemed to be a great many similarities between their lot and that of slaves. They had no property or legal rights of their own, could be separated from their children (as indeed happened to Wollstonecraft's own sister when she chose to leave her husband, resulting in the death of the child), could be locked up, and certainly could be raped or beaten with impunity by their husband, father or brothers.

Wollstonecraft's novel 'sequel' to *A Vindication*, *Maria, or the Wrongs of Women*, which was unfinished when she died, depicts many everyday situations in which it is clear that women are little more than slaves as far as society and the law are concerned. Her heroine, Maria, is an upper-middle-class woman who makes a bad marriage. Like Wollstonecraft herself, she is undervalued by her family, who prefer their son, tyrannized by her father, and given no property of her own. She then marries a man who turns out to be a libertine and makes her life a misery. There is marital rape, followed by unwanted pregnancy; she is sold to another man by her husband. When she finds that she cannot obtain legal separation, she escapes. When her husband finally catches up with her, he has her imprisoned in an asylum and takes her daughter away from her. The story of her jailor in the asylum, Jemima, is also told. An illegitimate child, she is made into a servant in her own father's household. She is raped, starved and beaten, then thrown out into the streets and forced into prostitution. As the heroine encounters other abused women, their stories are also told. All in all, it seems that Wollstonecraft did have good reasons to liken women to slaves – people with no rights of their own, who could be abused at will.

Yet, while Wollstonecraft did agree that many of her contemporaries were as slaves to their husband, father or society in general, in that they could not choose how to live their lives, whom to live it with, or even whom not to live it with, this is not what she is discussing in her Chapter Four. Just as she insists to Rousseau that she does not want women to be mistress of men, but only of themselves, what Wollstonecraft feels needs to be addressed urgently in this chapter is the ways in which women are enslaved to themselves: more precisely, to their senses (131). For example, she describes upper-class women as 'enervated' beings who 'seek for pleasure as the main purpose of their existence'. This is both because it is judged to be good for them, as women are supposed to be 'made to feel' in the same way that men are 'made to reason' (133), but also, conveniently, it panders to men's desires, leaving women with little to do but make themselves attractive to men, as if they were in a harem (144).

This commentary would have come as no surprise to eighteenth-century readers. It was deemed fashionable for women – and to some extent men[2] – to be that way, and the name for this fashionable condition was 'sensibility'. Women who have a high sensibility, Wollstonecraft tells us, are frightened by things as insignificant as mice (132), and rely on men to protect them from such terrors and to assist them in undemanding physical activities such as picking up a handkerchief, or holding a door open (126). Yet this weakness is regarded as attractive, and it appears to be in women's interest to cultivate it if they want to have any power over men. Women are taught to value 'sensibility', to develop a propensity for falling in love, gushing and crying a lot – what the French refer to as wearing one's emotions *a fleur de peau*, on the surface, visible to all, and ready to break out at any time. Sensibility, Wollstonecraft tells us, appealing to Samuel Johnson's definition, is 'quickness of sensation; quickness of perception; delicacy'.

Everything in the life of a well-off woman is pushing her towards sensibility: 'Novels, poetry and gallantry, all tend to make women the creatures of sensation, and their character is thus formed in the mold of folly during the time they are acquiring accomplishments, the only improvement they are excited, by their station in society, to acquire' (131). A few years later, this is brilliantly satirized by Jane Austen in *Sense and Sensibility*. As we saw in Chapter Four of this book, Austen's heroine, Marianne Dashwood, has many accomplishments, she believes her emotional responses to be of first importance in any judgment to be made, and she will not curb any of her enthusiasms or sudden distastes. In short, she is an insufferable, irrational creature, who clearly nevertheless has the capacity to be a sensible woman. At the end of the novel, she has the chance to reform and become more like her sister, Eleanor. But unlike the women Wollstonecraft is telling us about, Marianne was not systematically educated to become a slave to her senses – she merely picked up on what was fashionable and followed the not-so-good example of her mother. But she benefited from an otherwise sensible education, a kind father, and a sister who valued reason. Had she been in a position to marry the libertine Willoughby, whom she falls in love with at the beginning of the novel, it is likely that she would have only become worse, but heartbreak and near death bring her the chance to recover from her silliness.

But not only does 'sensibility' cause women to appear weak and to be treated as such – it does actually weaken their intellect, Wollstonecraft says. The senses are developed at the expense of reason. This is why, Wollstonecraft tells us, women are well and truly enslaved – unable to stop and contemplate what they are about to do, but simply following their inclinations:

> Their senses are inflamed, and their understanding neglected, consequently they become the prey of their senses, delicately termed sensibility, and are blown about by every momentary gust of feeling.

(130)

But just because Wollstonecraft claims that women are, in an important way, slaves to themselves, it does not follow that she thinks women are principally to blame for that situation. They are educated to obey their senses, and their reason is deliberately neglected. They are formed into the kind of beings that will please men. As Mill remarked nearly a century later, most men are not brutes: if they are to have slaves, they would rather they were willing slaves (Mill 1989: 132). The best way to achieve this result is to manipulate the consciousness of the person to be enslaved, and this, Wollstonecraft tells us, is what men have done to her contemporaries:

> Man, taking her body, the mind is left to rust; so that while physical love enervates man, as being his favourite recreation, he will endeavour to enslave woman: – and, who can tell, how many generations may be necessary to give vigour to the virtue and talents of the freed posterity of abject slaves?
>
> (148)

Women, Wollstonecraft reminds us (133), are rational creatures, so in order to flourish they need to be educated, their understanding needs to be strengthened in the only possible way: by giving them 'the power of generalising ideas, of drawing conclusions from individual observations' (123). So a good way for men to enslave women is simply to neglect to train their reason and to develop their senses in a way that actively prevents the growth of reason.

QUEENS IN CAGES

While discussing sensibility, it seems we moved rather strangely from slaves to aristocrats. This is exactly what Wollstonecraft does throughout her Chapter Four: women are compared with slaves, then tyrants, then slaves again. The metaphor of hereditary power is often used in *A Vindication*, and in a rather confusing way. On one hand, it is men's power that is responsible for keeping women uneducated and ultimately powerless, just as it is the power of kings and aristocrats that keeps the masses down. On the other hand, women are seen as holding a sort of pretend power, manifested in their appearance and the mock respect they receive from men, and this is compared with the supposed power of kings, who are bowed to but manipulated by their advisers. It is hard to see where one would place a married man or father in these distinctions, if he were not an aristocrat. In the same way, men are said to be both tyrants and slaves to women. If we look at the slavish aspect of women, then we will recognize that men are the tyrants to whom they answer, and if we consider women as queens in cages, then men are the grov-elling slaves who buy jewels, but at the same time keep the door to the cage locked. Let us look at the various parts of the metaphor in turn.

WOMEN AS SLAVES, MEN AS TYRANTS – THE REPUBLICAN ARGUMENT

As we saw in the previous section, Wollstonecraft says on several occasions that the condition of women is akin to slavery – not slavery in the obvious way that African people were slaves in Europe and the United States, but in a more subtle manner, without it being clearly stated. Women are made into willing slaves, the kind who do not wish to break free, because they believe their lot is a good one. So at the beginning of the chapter, Wollstonecraft compares women with serfs, who, rather than 'throwing off the yoke', do as they're told and carry on enjoying the small comforts and pleasures they are dealt. They are simply not interested in fighting back. Women, she says, had rather 'burnish their chains' than 'snap them' (124).

Wollstonecraft's characterization of women as slaves, and her claim that they will not break the chains of their own will, even though they are in part of their own making, is very much part of the republican rhetoric. It had to be noted that those that were to be freed from oppression seemed not to desire their freedom, that they had so far done little to obtain it, and this phenomenon had to be explained in such a way that it made it acceptable to force freedom on these willing slaves. Rousseau famously observed that 'enslaved people do nothing but boast of the peace and tranquility they enjoy in their chains'. By the time the French Revolution was in full swing, this tendency of the masses to adapt to slavery was recognized and accepted. As Condorcet wrote:

> It is in the power of habit to familiarize men with the violation of their natural rights to such a degree that, among those who have lost them, nobody ever thinks of reclaiming them or supposes himself to have suffered any wrong.
>
> (236)

Although the phenomenon is apparently the same in the case of the poor and of women, the case of women does present a slightly different problem. The republicans are fighting the kind of subservience that harms not just the willing slave, but those who enjoy enough freedom to want to change the system. So in the French Revolution, the middle classes were able to help the oppressed shake off the tyranny of the oppressors because it was in their interest to do so. But this cannot happen when there are only the oppressed and the oppressor. Rousseau's claim that we must be forced to be free will have no effect if there is no-one in whose interest it is to force slaves to be free.

One may reply that there are people in a position to help free women: Wollstonecraft herself, and those like her. Except that there don't seem to be enough women like her to make a real difference. She notes that 'even women of superior sense adopt the same sentiments' because of their 'fear of departing from a supposed sexual character' (122). And when she lists exceptional women who have broken free because they have benefited from a masculine education, only two are her contemporaries – Catherine Macaulay and Madame d'Eon; one of them – Macaulay – is dead, and the other – Madame d'Eon – is a French man dressing in women's clothes. So if Wollstonecraft wants to get together a group of British women to defend their contemporaries' rights, she may well end up being the only member. And whereas some men of her acquaintance agree with her feminist principles, she may well have felt that it would not be entirely in their interest to put these principles into practice.

So Wollstonecraft is very aware of the difficulty involved in finding someone to snap women's chains: 'I am afraid' she says 'that human nature is still in such a weak state that the abolition of titles, the corner stone of despotism, could only have been the work of men who had no titles to sacrifice' (48). As a result of this weakness, she feels it is unlikely that men will help women snap their chains,[3] and therefore that inequality should be combated gradually, not through a revolution, but by the few individuals such as herself who see the need for it, through rational persuasion of both oppressed and oppressor. This may take a long time: '[W]ho can tell, how many generations may be necessary to give vigour to the virtue and talents of the freed posterity of abject slaves?' (148). In this she echoes Kant, who wrote in his 'An answer to the question: what is enlightenment?':

> Thus a public can only attain enlightenment slowly. Perhaps a revolution can overthrow autocratic despotism and profiteering or power-grabbing oppression, but it can never truly reform a manner of thinking; instead, new prejudices, just like the old ones they replace, will serve as a leash for the great unthinking mass.
>
> (Reiss 1991: 55)

WOMEN AS QUEENS, MEN AS GROVELLING SLAVES

One reason why women will not snap their chains is that they do not see them. What they see is men's devotion to their person, and the apparent power they exercise over men. They see that they do not have to work, and can rely on men to provide them with security and luxury, provided they are pretty enough. 'It is true that they are provided with food and raiment, for which they neither toil nor spin' says Wollstonecraft of the woman in the cage (125). The role of these 'present gratifications', she tells us, is to incite women to forget that they have a soul, and that they should develop their understanding. But it is in part a mystery to her as to why it works: 'And why do they not discover, when "in the noon of beauty's power" that they are treated like queens only to be deluded by hollow respect, till they are led to resign or not assume their natural prerogatives?' (125). Part of the

answer to her own question is Wollstonecraft's analogy of women
with kings:

> A king is always a king – and a woman always a woman: his authority
> and her sex, ever stand between them and rational converse. [...]
> I lament that women are systematically degraded by receiving the trivial
> attentions, which men think it manly to pay to the sex, when, in fact, they
> are insultingly supporting their own superiority. It is not condescension
> to bow to an inferior.
>
> (126)

Whenever anyone is put on a pedestal, she says, a certain amount
of deception is involved – the person on the pedestal is made to
believe that they are superior and respected as such, but those
responsible for holding them on that pedestal know that is not so.
The king is useful to the aristocrats because he represents a strong
enough authority that the masses will respect the social order and
work for them. Women, we saw, are better slaves if they are
willing slaves, and the illusion of power achieves just this. That
no man was under the illusion that women really were queens is
made clear, I think, from reading the most ardent defender of
chivalry, Burke, when he writes of the effect of the Revolution,
when 'all the decent drapery of life is to be rudely torn off':

> On this scheme of things, a king is but a man; a queen is but a woman;
> a woman is but an animal; and an animal not of the highest order.

VOLUNTARY SUBMISSION 1: CONDORCET

In July 1790, the *Journal de La Société de 1789* published an article
by Condorcet entitled '*Sur l'admission des femmes au droit de la cité*',[4]
in which he argued that it was a gross injustice, an act of tyranny,
for women not to be granted equal rights to men. As we saw in
Chapter Two of this book, the early days of the French Revolution were a good time for the few hopefuls defending women's
rights: equality was on everyone's minds, and there were many
women actively defending the Revolution, both in the streets and in
salons. A few put their hopes in writing, and actually attempted to

convince the Assembly to grant women full citizen rights. Of course, they failed, and during the terror women's movements were severely repressed.

Condorcet's argument for granting women rights is a simple one: unless there are good reasons why women should not be granted citizenship, then their exclusion is an act of tyranny. There could only be two kinds of good reason: 'that the natural rights of women are not absolutely identical with those of men' or 'that women are incapable of exercising them' (Morley 1995: 237) On the first point, Condorcet's attitude is identical to Wollstonecraft's. Rights, he says, are derived from the 'capacity of acquiring moral ideas, and of reasoning on those ideas' (*ibid.*: 237). Because women have these capabilities, their natural rights are the same as those of men, he concludes.

Refuting the second reason requires more argument on his part. First, he examines the claim that women have not as much intelligence as men, because 'no woman has made an important discovery in science, nor given proof of genius in arts, literature, etc.' Of course, we know better now, but Condorcet makes the very good point that the possible intellectual superiority of a few inventors, artists or writers does not make for the superiority of men over women. He then considers two more points and discusses them extremely briefly: first, that women do not follow reason; second, that they do not have the 'sentiment of justice'. Women do follow reason, he says – but they follow their own, not men's:

> Their interests not being the same by defect of the laws, and the same things not having for them the same importance as for us, they may without failing in reason, make up their minds on other principles, and aim at a different end. It is not more unreasonable for a woman to take pains about her personal appearance than it was for Demosthenes to take pains with his voice and his gesticulation.
>
> (*ibid.*: 239)

To the claim that women do not have the sentiment of justice, Condorcet replies that 'It is not nature, it is education, it is the manner of social life, which is the cause of this difference' (*ibid.*: 239). As to the 'sensitive nature' of women, and their ensuing inability to understand a concept as harsh as justice, Condorcet is then in perfect agreement with Wollstonecraft. Sensitive is not what women are by nature, it is what men want them to be, and if little girls were educated to understand and value justice more than they value their 'feelings', there would be no difference between them and men. Wollstonecraft adds to this that boys would benefit from learning more sensitivity (not the dreaded sensibility that she denigrates in her contemporaries, but the cultivation of family affections) by attending day schools rather than being sent away to school, so that they may benefit from the warmth of family life.

Wollstonecraft may agree with Condorcet that justice is common to men and women, and that any difference between the sexes in their aptitude for citizenship is a matter of education, but she would, I think, disagree with him that women simply have to redirect their reason to political ends to become as reasonable as men. Condorcet seems to assume that, were women to be granted the right to be politically active, we would see straightaway that there was nothing wrong with their reasoning capacities. They have simply been using them differently, in spheres where men may not have noticed them. Running a home, bringing up children, holding one's place in society all require as much reasoning as being politically active. But this reasoning is not apparent to those who know nothing of the workings of a home or polite society: it is then just assumed that women do not reason. Although this is an attractive view, it has one weakness, namely that it fails to account for women's lack of desire to claim for themselves the rights that are naturally theirs. When Olympe de Gouges, in her *Declaration of the Rights of Woman* enjoins her contemporaries to 'wake up [...] discover your rights', she is not immediately answered by a large number of women wanting to claim their rights. French women, it seems, although willing to take to the streets and their salons to abolish the tyranny of monarchy, were not as passionate about abolishing the tyranny of patriarchy. Wollstonecraft argues that one of the reasons behind women's unwillingness to 'wake up' and claim their rights is that the uneducated or badly educated and 'enslaved' woman has few reasoning skills – those she needs to be pretty and cunning, but not those she needs to discuss politics intelligently. This is not something she believes to be the case for all her contemporaries. It would be fairer to say that, rather than simply the lack of education, she blames the wrong kind of education: at the end of her Chapter Four, she remarks that:

> Indeed, the good sense which I have met with, among the poor women who have had few advantages of education, and yet have acted heroically, strongly confirmed me in the opinion that trifling employments have rendered woman a trifler. Man, taking her body, has left her mind to rust.

(148)

But it is those women with the leisure and the social influence to claim rights for themselves whose minds are 'rusted'. Those who can reason as well as men are uneducated and poor, so have neither leisure nor influence. So as far as Wollstonecraft is concerned, arguments such as Condorcet puts forward fail to address the issue: offer women the rights of citizenship, she says, and they will not want them, they will declare themselves incompetent and uninterested. First, we need to change women's attitudes: teach them that their own liberty is desirable. What Condorcet seems to underestimate, compared with Wollstonecraft, is the power of habituation, which has made wealthy women into 'triflers' and means that they cannot suddenly become free-thinking citizens. For Wollstonecraft, in order for an adult to be a fully functioning citizen, she or he must have been habituated into that role, that is, received an appropriate education from early childhood onwards. That is the crux of Wollstonecraft's implicit disagreement with Condorcet.

VOLUNTARY SUBMISSION 2: MILL

For Wollstonecraft, it seems that the reason women do not wish for freedom is that their preference for servitude is formed for them, from the very beginning, by men who intend to make them their slaves. Men 'endeavour to enslave woman' (148) and they do so by teaching them 'from their infancy that beauty is woman's scepter' as a result of which 'the mind shapes itself to the body, and,

roaming around its gilt cage, only seeks to adorn its prison' (112).
Small pleasures are dished out to occupy women's minds – 'she is
incited by present gratification to forget her grand destination' (133).
This education ensures the stunted growth of women's minds,
and enslaves them: 'Thus degraded, her reason, her misty reason! is
employed rather to burnish than to snap her chains' (176). In this
respect, her views seem very close indeed to what Mill argued,
nearly a century later, in his essay 'The Subjection of Women':

> in the case of women a hot-house and stove cultivation has always
> been carried on some of the capabilities of their nature, for the ben-
> efit of their masters. Then because certain products of the general
> vital force sprout luxuriantly and reach a great development in this
> heated atmosphere and under this active nurture and watering, while
> other shoots from the same root, which are left outside, in the wintry
> air, with ice purposefully heaped all around them, have a stunted
> growth, and some are burnt off with fire and disappear ...
>
> (Mill 1989: 139)

Given the closeness in their views, it is very surprising that Mill
does not, at any point, refer to Wollstonecraft. Perhaps one
explanation was Wollstonecraft's fall from favour after her death
and the revelations her husband made about her life, which, in
the nineteenth century, robbed her of respectability and therefore
credibility. At the time when Mill wrote, she was far from being
as widely read as she had been in her lifetime. But it still seems
that a serious philosopher working on the condition of women
would have troubled to find out, and that this would have resulted
in some sort of acknowledgment.

Mill and Wollstonecraft share the suggestion that women's
capacity to flourish is manipulated from the very beginning. That
is, not only are they not prepared for a fully human life, but their
natural dispositions towards such a life are thwarted. Mill and
Wollstonecraft even use the same gardening analogy – that of the
hot-house – to express that view.[5] This is a common enough analogy, and Wollstonecraft's contemporaries would have been used to
hearing of the cultivation of the woman's mind, either through
comparisons of women with pretty flowers (Barbauld: 'Gay without

toil, lovely without art, [...] Your BEST, your SWEETEST empire is – TO PLEASE'; Burke also draws this comparison in his essay on the sublime); with decadent, showy flowers (Pope's claim that women, like tulips, are 'fine by defect'; Swift's famous line 'such gaudy tulips raised from dung') – or of Rousseau's advice that women should refrain from too much cultivation and be as close as possible to nature.[6]

As far as both Mill and Wollstonecraft are concerned, the growth of women's rational and moral abilities is stunted, and the growth of their feminine attributes, such as they are perceived in the two philosophers' respective centuries, are unnaturally enhanced through 'hot-house' cultivation. But it seems that Wollstonecraft and Mill nonetheless differ in their analysis of why this systematic distortion of women's capabilities occurs in the first place. Mill seems to believe that there is an almost conscious manipulation of women's capabilities by men. Men want slaves, if possible willing slaves, who will serve without resentment and without any prompt from their masters.

> All men, except perhaps the most brutish, desire to have, in the woman most nearly connected with them, not a forced slave but a willing one [... So men have] put everything in practice to enslave their minds.
>
> (Mill 1989: 132)

Frances Power Cobbe, a contemporary of Mill, in her review of 'The Subjection of Women' felt that Mill did not emphasize this aspect of women's oppression sufficiently (Cobbe 1869/1995: 54–74). She talks of the unnatural aspect of 'the characters and abilities of creatures manipulated as women are' (*ibid.*: 60) and describes the process of the manipulation as follows. 'She may freely grow, and even swell to abnormal proportions in the region of the heart; but the head has but a small chance of expansion and the whole base is weak and rickety to the extreme' (*ibid.*: 61). For Cobbe, what men did to women was analogous to a practice rumoured to have taken place in medieval China, that of placing infants into jars and letting them grow there, so that they take on amusing distorted forms.

The idea that men deliberately manipulate women as they would an exotic flower, so as to maximize the pleasing effects whilst minimizing the inconvenience, is somewhat dubious. One is reminded of the 1975 Bryan Forbes film *The Stepford Wives*, in which the men of a small town club together to robotize their wives, thereby ensuring that they conform to their ideal of what women should be like and become, literally, willing slaves. But such systematic manipulation is unlikely to be the result of conscious conspiracy. For such a scenario to be in place, men would first have to be aware that women are capable of wanting similar things out of life as men do; then realize that they could effect certain changes to women's desires that would be to men's, but not to women's, advantage; then cooperate to effect those changes. It does seem unlikely that men, as group, would go through such a mental process. It would require an unlikely degree of cooperation and of sheer bad will on the part of men.

It does not seem that Wollstonecraft shares in this conspiracy theory. What she does clearly believe is that at least as significant as the habituation to frivolity in the shaping of her contemporaries' consciousness is the lack of formal education, which she discusses in *A Vindication* but also in her first book, *On the Education of Daughters*. Whereas boys are taught formally from an early age, women 'receive only a disorderly kind of education'. In particular, women are not trained to apply themselves to detail, or 'with exactness', and develop no sense of method. What they acquire instead is 'a negligent kind of guesswork' which leads to an inability to 'generalize matters of fact' (88). Wollstonecraft emphasizes that early education is the only remedy to this defect as 'a child very soon contracts a benumbing indolence of mind, which, he has seldom sufficient vigour afterwards to shake off' (241).

Another factor in women's apparent inability to mature intellectually is a tendency to leave little girls in the care of an ignorant nurse, who will 'humour all her little caprices' (Wollstonecraft 1994: 5) and encourage them to become gossips (*ibid*.: 109). Also relevant is the fact that girls and young women are not engaged in any serious activity that would 'silence their feelings' and allow their minds to become stronger (Wollstonecraft 1999/1792: 146). Instead, Wollstonecraft says, 'trifling employments have rendered woman a trifler' (*ibid*.: 148).

Last but not least, Wollstonecraft blames early marriage, because it prevents a woman's mind from having the proper time to digest the education it has received and to mature (Wollstonecraft 1994: 93–94). Early marriage also takes away the advantages men derive from 'being obliged to struggle with the world', such as seeing human nature 'as it is' rather than living purely in their imagination, as women who leave their parents' home only to become wives and mothers tend to do (*ibid.*: 100).

The cumulative effect of this neglect of women's education is likely, eventually, to be very similar to Mill's conspiracy theory: women fail to develop strong reasoning skills, virtuous character, proper concern for others and wider interests. They are concerned with little other than dress and gossip. Note that Wollstonecraft does not believe the only thing that is holding her contemporaries back is vanity. She has much to say about the lot of poorer women coping single-handedly with hordes of dependents while their husbands do little to help them; or women forced into prostitution because there is a market for it, and no other profession open to them that would enable them to support themselves when no-one else can. But Wollstonecraft does not claim, and she is right not to, that such women would not welcome change were it offered to them. Her target, and the object of the arguments I have just described, is the class of women who are sufficiently well off to be supported in idleness by their male relatives.

WOLLSTONECRAFT AND SEN'S ADAPTIVE PREFERENCES

The phenomenon Wollstonecraft describes and tries to explain pre-empts in many ways philosopher and economist Amartya Sen's concept of adaptive preferences, sometimes also referred to as 'sour grapes', a concept that has played a very important role in our understanding of world poverty and our reflections on how it might be remedied. In *Inequality Re-examined*, Sen describes the phenomenon of adaptive preferences as follows:

> A thoroughly deprived person, leading a very reduced life, might not appear to be badly off in terms of the mental metric of desire and its

fulfillment, if the hardship is accepted with non grumbling resignation. In situations of long standing deprivation, the victims do not go on grieving and lamenting all the time, and very often make great effort to take pleasure in small mercies and to cut down personal desires to modest – 'realistic' – proportions.

(Sen 1992: 55)

Sen's theory is based in great part on his own observations of how the destitute and the oppressed tend to describe their own wellbeing. If, for instance, the inhabitants of a comparatively well-off region of India, Kerala, complain of ill health more than the inhabitants of a poorer region, Bihar, there is likely more to the explanation than that the poor are more resistant to illness than the rich (Sen 2006: 88). Sen's explanation is that where standards of healthcare are known to be low, people tend to complain less. Faced with necessary deprivation, people need to forget the gap in their life; they need, for the sake of survival, to became convinced that it was never there. This is how, in another of Sen's examples, women in rural India came to believe that their nutritional needs were close to non-existent, and in any case inferior to those of their husbands and children.

Sen's identification of this phenomenon led him to reject measurements of wellbeing based on satisfaction. Because preferences are malleable, being satisfied with one's lot is not a reliable way to measure wellbeing (with a view to distributing resources). People learn to live with what they can get, and do not waste energy wishing they could get what is unavailable to them. This phenomenon has also been described as 'sour grapes' after Aesop's fable in which a fox decides that he does not desire the grapes he cannot reach, and tells himself, knowing that it is false, that they were sour anyway.[7]

There is nonetheless an important and illuminating difference between Sen's adaptive preferences and the phenomenon described by Wollstonecraft. For Wollstonecraft, women are programmed from their youth to prefer things that are not truly advantageous for them. They do not grow up loving freedom, and then trick themselves into believing they no longer desire it once it becomes apparent that it will be taken away from them. Nor is their love for 'small comforts' in any way false. It is not what women ought to prefer, it is not good for them to prefer it, but their preference is nonetheless genuine.

Sen has said that he owes some of his thoughts on adaptive preferences to Wollstonecraft, but it seems he has not quite understood what Wollstonecraft is claiming.[8] If he had, he might have been in a position to distinguish between two different kinds of phenomena that take place alongside each other. People for whom obtaining food is difficult, he says, are prepared to believe that they are not underfed when they clearly are. This could be a case of either adaptive preferences, or the stunted growth of preferences such as Wollstonecraft describes, depending on whether or not the people in question have suffered from malnutrition for most of their lives. If not, then they presumably adapted their preferences from believing they needed a certain quantity of food, to believing they needed less. But Sen himself notes that in such cases, women are liable to claim they need even less then their menfolk. This can only be explained if these women have a propensity to believe that they are 'lower maintenance' or less important than men – it seems unlikely that men and women would otherwise respond differently to famine – unless it were the case that women's nutritional requirements truly were significantly lower than men's, which, especially in cases where women do as much work as men and care for children, is certainly not the case.

As illuminating as Sen's concept of adaptive preferences is, it seems it is more so if we take into account what Wollstonecraft has to say on the subject of why women do not fight oppression when they could do so. Her arguments reinforce the view already held, that education is the first requirement in helping people help themselves. In the case of women in deprived parts of the world, Wollstonecraft would argue that they need to be educated in order to come to value their own lives, and to understand what they would be capable of as citizens. Although a lot of Wollstonecraft's arguments are addressed to women of leisure, and although she would almost certainly address lower-caste Indian women of today in a very different tone from that she uses for her contemporaries, the 'triflers', no doubt she would feel her arguments were useful there too.

CONCLUSION

It is clear that the notion of habituation plays a very important role in Wollstonecraft's diagnosis of her contemporaries' situation. Virtues that are needed to achieve citizenship and to live a fully human life need to be developed through habitual behaviour. A woman who has had a haphazard education will not have developed these virtues. One who has received an education that emphasizes 'trifles', such as gossip, embroidery, etc., will become a trifler. But also to be virtuous is to be wise, and someone who has been deprived of wisdom will not be virtuous – will not even see that virtue is desirable. This, according to Wollstonecraft, explains why her contemporaries do not seek to better themselves, or to emancipate themselves: they are ignorant of what they are missing.

6

ANGELS AND BEASTS

In this chapter I discuss Chapter Five of *A Vindication*, entitled 'Animadversions on some of the writers who have rendered women objects of pity, bordering on contempt'. There Wollstonecraft responds to claims and arguments made in writings on women, some by male writers and some by female ones. In the discussion of this chapter, I attempt to determine what would have been Wollstonecraft's responses to feminist, anti-feminist and proto-feminist literature written around or before her time, largely focusing on her animadversions, but not exclusively so. In particular, I do not discuss here Madame de Genlis' thoughts on obedience, as these will be better placed in Chapter Eight, which deals with Wollstonecraft's views on the family. The Baroness de Stael is discussed at the same time as Rousseau, as Wollstonecraft seems to believe she does little but repeat him. I will not say much about Fordyce, Gregory, Piozzi or Chapone, and nothing at all about Chesterfield – I do not feel that a discussion of their views would add significantly to our understanding of Wollstonecraft's arguments here. On the other hand, I add short discussions of Mary Astell and Hannah More, both writers of a Tory persuasion whom Wollstonecraft does not mention, but whose views add significance to the debate. At the end of this chapter, I try and situate Wollstonecraft within twenty-first-century feminist philosophy, focusing particularly on the question as to whether universalism is always patriarchal and whether it makes sense to focus on difference.

A CROSS BETWEEN A RANT AND A LITERATURE REVIEW

To the twenty-first-century eye, the structure of Chapter Five of *A Vindication* is difficult to follow. It is longer than any of the previous chapters, and unlike them it is divided into sections. It is not clear what the rationale for the division is. The first section talks of Rousseau only, the second Dr Fordyce, the third Gregory, the fourth covers several female writers: Hester Piozzi, Baroness de Stael, Madame Genlis, Mrs Chapone and Catherine Macaulay. The final section considers Chesterfield's claim that a good education should entail an early awareness of 'the ways of the world'. Wollstonecraft expresses her distaste of this view and ridicules it at length.

Each section contains either long quotations or short summaries of the texts discussed, followed by a refutation, sometimes consisting of little but the pouring of scorn over another writer. Overall, the chapter feels to us who are not used to this particular style of writing like a cross between a rant and a literature review. But it is exactly as it is meant to be: a putting forward and refutation of the available opposing theories. Chapter Five follows a literary genre common to renaissance revivals of classical rhetorical styles. Animadversions were a common rhetorical device of antiquity, and still in use in the seventeenth and eighteenth centuries – a method for responding to objections, typically consisting of quotations followed by responses. Leibniz used the genre in this way, but also by writing imaginary dialogues with his opponents in several works.[1] Wollstonecraft would probably have inherited the style from Milton, who used it in his prose writings, in particular the pamphlets of 1649.[2] We know from the fact that he is quoted in *A Vindication* that she was familiar with at least some of his writings – and we ought not to be surprised by this, as Milton was a republican and generally much loved by the republican thinkers of eighteenth-century England.[3]

ROUSSEAU AND MADAME DE STAEL

Although women had been writing seriously on education for a while, it was still, in the late eighteenth century, male writers who were being cited and followed as far as the education of girls was concerned. The most famous was Rousseau, but treatises by Fordyce and Gregory were also widely read (the awful Mr Collins in Jane Austen's *Pride and Prejudice* insists on reading from Fordyce to the Bennett girls). This explains, at least in part, why Wollstonecraft spends most of her chapter on animadversions criticizing the works of men – they would have seemed to her, and to everyone else, more serious opponents. I shall begin this section by discussing her responses to the most influential of those educators: Jean-Jacques Rousseau.

Throughout her career, Wollstonecraft compared herself and her views with Rousseau's. He was her yardstick, the writer she could both admire and despise, someone she could compete with in her mind. She was a strong admirer of his works, both his political writings and his views on education. She reviewed his *Confessions* for the *Analytical Review* in April 1790, six months before she wrote the first *Vindication*, and a year and a half before she started writing the second. This review is longer than what she typically wrote, witnessing her fascination with Rousseau's life and character. He is a genius, she says, and yet she refrains from formulating a judgment of his worth as a philosopher, preferring readers to form their own judgment.

What we know from other writings is that Wollstonecraft felt that Rousseau's works displayed the right balance of intellectual rigour and emotional sincerity, and she tried to emulate this in her own writings. Her very first published work, *Mary*, was a semi-autobiographical novel intended, like *Emile* and the *Confessions*, to disseminate her views on education and politics. While she was in Paris, a year after writing *A Vindication*, she confessed to her partner that she had always been 'half in love' with Rousseau. This admiration she felt for Rousseau and his work may bring some perspective on her vehement attack on Rousseau's views in *A Vindication*, and in particular in the chapter on the animadversions. She would have expected a writer whose work she so admired to get the question of women's education right. That he didn't was not only incredibly difficult to understand – just as we find it incredibly difficult to understand how Aristotle could have got the question of slavery so very wrong – but also a betrayal. As a philosopher who was also a woman, she expected more from Rousseau.

Wollstonecraft spends a third of her Chapter Five discussing the section of *Emile* that relates to the education of women, at times systematically refuting Rousseau's views, setting out his arguments and displaying their weaknesses, the rest of the time simply ridiculing or exclaiming against the sheer stupidity of some of his claims.

> Sophie must be a woman as Emile is a man, that is, she must have all that belongs to the constitution of her species and her sex in order to take her place in the physical and moral order. Let us therefore begin by examining the ways in which her sex contrasts and compares to ours.

These are the opening words of the Fifth book of *Emile* (Rousseau 1992: 445).[4] Note that the woman is contrasted with the readers, who are assumed to be male. Note also that Rousseau is assuming that sexual differences are of the same order as differences between species: that they are therefore natural and essential.

As he describes what he takes to be the difference between men and women in a few short paragraphs, he feels able to conclude almost immediately that 'woman is made specially to please man'. Because the sexes must contribute to the common good in different ways, according to their different nature, it also follows, he says, that men ought to be 'active and strong', and women 'passive and weak'. It is not surprising, I feel, that Wollstonecraft should have experienced a degree of impatience when confronted by arguments at once so sloppy and outrageous. These claims are simply asserted in the first two pages of the text, and Rousseau clearly feels he has argued for them sufficiently to be able to go on to describe what the education of these 'weak and passive' creatures ought to be. So he tells us in the very next paragraph: 'If woman is made to please and be subjugated, she ought to make herself agreeable to man' (*ibid.*: 446).

A few pages later, Rousseau feels he has sufficiently argued his case for the natural disparity of the sexes, including the fact that the 'proper purpose' of women is to 'produce children', so he is able to conclude the following:

> Once it is demonstrated that man and woman are not and ought not to be constituted in the same way in either character or temperament, it follows that they ought not to have the same education.
>
> (*ibid.*: 453)

One can relate to Wollstonecraft's frustration here. A man whose writings on education she greatly admires, and after whom she models her own philosophical persona, a man who will be greatly influential in the new directions of education in republican France, is saying that there must not be any equality in the education of boys and girls, but that on the contrary, we must perpetuate and maybe even strengthen the very gender roles that Wollstonecraft is fighting against.

The particulars of what Rousseau proposes concerning women's education, and of the corresponding aspects of woman's nature, are what Wollstonecraft finds particularly offensive. Women, he says, must be taught from an early age to make themselves beautiful. They must learn to make dresses, embroider, and perfect the art of looking attractive while appearing chaste and modest. Most of all, they must learn to master the art of looking good. But women must not complain that they are forced to engage in these trivial matters, for, Rousseau says, no-one forces them to. Women are in charge of educating girls, and if they did not think dress and appearance were important, they would not teach them to their daughters. Women do not go to university, he says, and therefore they are free to be educated sensibly, in a way that fits their nature, and not forced to learn things that will enhance their intellect artificially.

In fact, he suggests, women simply would not be able to attend to a university education. Their minds are not capable of the level of abstract thought that would be required, and they use language not to express linear thoughts, but to gossip. In other words, what Wollstonecraft sees as a deformation of women's natural intellectual capacities, Rousseau sees as a true expression of what befits them.

Madame de Stael, whom Wollstonecraft sees as little more than a sycophant, claims that Rousseau is right but does not go far enough. By preventing women from claiming equality with men, he is, she says, helping them reclaim their own nature, and therefore giving them the ability to flourish as they should, rather than wither in a position that is not truly theirs. But if women are weak by nature, she says, they will need virtues that are less useful to men in order to flourish. So they will need more 'strength of soul' than men, to make up for their natural inferiority and to make themselves more palatable partners for their husbands.

That Rousseau was a man of sensibility – and a womanizer – did nothing to harm his image with intellectual women of his time. It may seem surprising, however, to see an intelligent, educated woman thank him for re-establishing the natural order by telling women they ought not to shine in politics. Madame de Stael was, after all, herself in the centre of political life – so much so that Bonaparte felt he had to exile her. So why should she have been in such perfect agreement with Rousseau's views, which were incompatible with the way in which she led her life?[5]

Rousseau appeals to *love* as women's empire. And he claims that through love, through their powers of attraction, women are in fact the true masters, even though in appearance it is men who are on top. Because women, as he says, have more power of attraction over men than men have over women, and because a man may never know if a woman gives herself to him because she wants to or because he is more powerful, Rousseau thinks men are under women's power.

Wollstonecraft's response to this is simply that 'When women are once sufficiently enlightened to discover their real interest, on a grand scale, they will, I am persuaded, be very ready to resign all the prerogatives of love, that are not mutual, speaking of them as lasting prerogatives, for the calm satisfaction of friendship, and the tender confidence of habitual esteem' (Wollstonecraft 1999/1792: 179). In other words, women are being tricked when they are led to believe that being a mistress in love matters more than the rest, and a little general education should suffice to show this. But this does not explain why an educated woman such as de Stael does not see things in this way.

What Wollstonecraft does not tell us, for the sake of decorum perhaps, is that as a woman she is fully aware that attraction works both ways, and that she does not have magical powers that hold men in her sway. For a woman like de Stael, who was rich and by all accounts a natural flirt, things may have seemed different. But a middle-class woman who has to work and be respectable at the same time cannot behave in the same way as a French aristocrat, and therefore these considerations do not apply to her.

But whether even Rousseau was aware that women, too, could feel the attraction of the opposite sex (or the same sex for that matter) is irrelevant insofar as Rousseau, as well as most of his contemporaries, held that appearances and reputation had to be maintained at all costs by women. Rousseau does not expect women to be naturally chaste – they are, after all, creatures of pleasure rather than reason. Nor does he expect a woman to find self-control in religious faith: her religious beliefs must be no more than what her husband advises her to believe. All her efforts in learning should be directed towards becoming more attractive, Rousseau says, and an English woman ought to pay as much attention to her appearance as a Circassian woman in a harem would (159). As far as morality and religion are concerned, they need not trouble themselves: 'Your husband will instruct you in good time'. It follows that any chastity displayed by a woman in Rousseau's view will be merely superficial.

Wollstonecraft is quick to point out this inconsistency, in Rousseau and other male writers, of advice to women: chastity is valued and deemed necessary, but women are not capable of virtue and therefore cannot show anything more than superficial chastity at best, and lie to preserve a reputation for chastity at worst. Dr Fordyce, who is discussed in Section II of the Animadversions, even goes so far as to suggest that a pious woman is more attractive, and that therefore, if a woman wants to catch her husband, she should cultivate a look of piety. Wollstonecraft, unsurprisingly, has very little time for either the hypocrisy which claims that men prefer demure women, or the recommendation that women cultivate religion so as to gain power over men.

Although Dr Gregory, whose work is discussed in Section III, seems also to be of the opinion that women need to dissimulate and that they should 'be cautious when displaying your good sense', unlike Rousseau and Fordyce he is honest enough that he realizes and says that women must only appear stupid and weak if they want to find a husband and a good place in society. That is, he respects women just enough to explain to them rationally why it is in their interest to cultivate an air of ignorance and stupidity. But Wollstonecraft, although she does find Gregory less objectively outrageous than Rousseau or Fordyce, still objects strongly to what she calls a 'system of dissimulation', whereby girls made of flesh and bone are taught to appear as weak, saintly objects for the sole purpose of finding a husband who can provide for them in a society where they cannot provide for themselves.

The overall picture one gets from the authors Wollstonecraft discusses in the first three sections of the Animadversions is a very incoherent one indeed. Women are creatures of pleasure, but they are not predators. Their lives are not ruled by an urge to seek gratification. Instead of being predators, they are themselves hunted, by men, who are supposed to be ruled by reason rather than desires, but who somehow fall victims to attraction in a way that women cannot. But because women are creatures of desire, they cannot reason, and they cannot become truly virtuous, but must obey superior beings – men – in all things. In order to obey, they must develop superior virtues to those of men. Also, because women are supposed to be weak, they can do nothing but let themselves be hunted, and once they have been caught, attempt to retain their position. But this, somehow, is a sign of their power over men.

I think it is fair to say that Wollstonecraft would have succeeded, in these three sections, in publicly ridiculing those male authors who claim to educate women. She would have shown that their views are laden with inconsistencies, non-sequiturs and contradictions, and that rather than prove that men are rational and women are not, they each demonstrate that they themselves fail to be rational when writing about women, and hence should not be taken seriously on that subject.

THE WOMEN – THE CONSERVATIVES AND THE REPUBLICANS

In the Animadversions, Wollstonecraft pours scorn on writings on female morality by both men and women. The men, we saw, seem to be unable to apply the rules of logic to what they have to say about women. Women, on the other hand, apart from those few who agree with her, are selling out, protecting their reputation, or just being plain silly.

> Indignantly have I heard women argue in the same tracks as men, and adopt the sentiments that brutalise them, with all the pertinacity of ignorance.
>
> (176)

She then proceeds to argue against most of her female contemporaries. Of Mrs Piozzi, a friend of Dr Johnson, she says that she 'often repeated by rote, what she did not understand' (176). Of Madame Genlis, she says that 'her views are narrow, and her prejudices as unreasonable as strong' (179). She concludes the section by referring to the one woman writer she wholly admires, Catherine Macaulay, who is remarkable for both the rightness of her views and her general intellectual achievements:

> I will not call hers a masculine understanding, because I admit not of such an arrogant assumption of reason; but I contend that it was a sound one, that her judgment, the matured fruit of profound thinking, was a proof that a woman can acquire judgment, in the full extent of the word.
>
> (180)

Although now we mostly agree with Wollstonecraft's analyses, it may feel strange that she is basically disagreeing with all but one of her contemporaries. She may well feel that such stern disagreement is needed. She is shaking them all and saying: 'Look, women are oppressed, no better than slaves, and you are all contributing to their condition!'. Yet very few rallied to her call, very few felt vindicated by what she had to say. Wollstonecraft had a theory about why they wouldn't – they had been educated into slavery, brought up to value their dependence and whatever small advantages it brought them. 'How few! – how very few! have sufficient foresight, or resolution, to endure a small evil a the moment, to avoid a greater hereafter' (176). So it was guaranteed that until little girls were educated differently, women would not demand to have rights, and would not fight for their own liberty.

However convincing Wollstonecraft's account may be for the majority of middle-class or aristocratic women, it does not explain why other educated women who were also politically engaged and writing professionally did not agree with her. Some of these women appear to have genuinely valued their femininity and the difference in social status that went with it – for someone like Anna Laetitia Barbauld, her contemporary and a member of the same social and intellectual circles, grace, subtlety, softness are surer weapons for a woman than rights, ensuring that her voice is heard and that she gets what she deserves.[6]

As a republican, Barbauld was concerned with injustice, but it seems that she put most injustice against women down to poverty and social inferiority. If a man is treated well by society, she seems to think, he will treat his wife as well as she deserves. She was convinced that women were essentially different, that their reason did not operate in the same way as that of men, so that, for instance, most little girls would be able to 'learn by rote' (by heart), but not be suited to 'investigations'. Presumably she regarded herself as an exception. She was in many ways exceptional: not many people, men or women, can become acclaimed poets, as she did, but she did not expect to find her mental abilities in other women. They should be content with qualities that Barbauld felt all women did have – qualities of grace, softness and fragility – and the ability to use these qualities to persuade and to get one's own way. Quite why she felt that these qualities were any more universal among women than rational qualities is unclear. Surely she would have come across many women who were not naturally graceful, fragile or charming in any way, just as she would have come across women who were not very good at reasoning. But Barbauld, who had what she considered both feminine and masculine qualities, felt qualified to decide which were which, and to impose on her contemporaries certain standards – her message is clear: be a flower, or be a failure! And if you choose to develop your reason at the expense of your charms, you will be unnatural and unhappy.

One way to interpret thinkers such as Barbauld is as rejecting a patriarchal sort of universalism. Men are superior only according to their own standards, they would say, but women can be perceived as just as valuable, once we realize that there is more than one standard, more than one way of being powerful and strong. So, in a sense, Barbauld could be seen as advocating a sort of difference feminism, and rejecting the kind of feminism that seeks to make women more like men. Why shouldn't we value women for what they are, value their different sorts of contributions to society, respect their natural qualities and seek to enhance them, rather than always compare with men, and therefore see them as inferior rather than different? But it feels as though Barbauld is not so much putting value on difference, as putting forward a second set of universal values and imposing them on women. For her, a woman who is not relying on her looks to get ahead is not a successful woman. Nor is a woman of strong intellect who seeks to compete with men. A woman's nature is to love, and if she tries instead to let herself be led by cold intellect, she will soon find that nature calls her back to softness.

The kind of difference feminism Barbauld is advocating is not liberating. She imposes on women her perceptions of male and female nature, and does not allow much cross-over at all. She is not, as some feminists have done in the past fifty years, acknowledging that there is more than one way, typically the male way, to live a successful, valuable life – but she is saying that there are exactly two ways, one for men and one for women, and this is more oppressive than even a patriarchal universalism.

The view that women should be valued for their difference, and that this includes lack of intellectual abilities, is one reason why some women disagreed with Wollstonecraft, but by no means the only reason. For other women, the reason may simply have been that revolutions and social reform seemed too uncertain and too violent to be relied on. It certainly seems to be the case for an early feminist writer, Mary Astell, who, as a Tory in the first half of the eighteenth century, recommended that women do not step out of their position and remain obedient to their husbands, even if they be educated. She held this view despite the fact that she thought marriage was, on the whole, not advantageous to women. It may well be the case that Astell and other writers in favour of the *status quo* simply did not believe that change for the better was possible. To such women, Wollstonecraft would have appeared dangerous, risking everything for a dream. It may have seemed a lot more sensible to push for reforms within the system: to accept that women should have subordinate roles, but to push for them to be educated better than they currently were, and to be contented with their lot.

Hannah More and Mary Astell are both prime examples of this way of thinking. For Astell, there was no question that women could benefit from marriage, or that they should try and get out of it or change the rules of marriage so as to make it a more comfortable experience for all. Women should accept that they are subservient to their husbands. But what they can do, Astell tells us, is better their chances of being happy in the after-life. Educating children to be good Christians, she says, is a worthwhile activity that will earn them a place in heaven. But to be able to do this, women need a solid education, an education that will also make married life easier to bear, because it will give women a richer inner life and greater stocks of patience. So it was possible for Astell both to ask women not to try and better their social conditions, and to push for better schooling for them. She in fact recommended, and very nearly implemented, a Platonic Academy for women.

Hannah More's negative personal response to Wollstonecraft can also be understood in terms of her attitude to poverty. In response to the French Revolution, More published a large number of tracts encouraging the poor of England to love religion, to develop patience and contentment, and to hate revolutions and the French. But at the same time she was an active philanthropist, opening schools and helping the poor in various practical ways.

The uncharitable interpretations of women such as Astell and More would be to say, as Wollstonecraft might, that they are only seeking to benefit the oppressed so that they will not turn against their oppressors and allow the oppression to carry on unchallenged. But a more charitable interpretation, which fits these writers' obvious concerns for humanity, is to say that they simply did not believe that revolutionary change was possible, and therefore sought to discourage it and to encourage instead improvements that they thought were a real possibility. Immediate historical events did back up this attitude. French women who had hoped for equality of rights under the new regime soon found themselves harshly pushed back into subservience. Olympe de Gouges and Madame Roland were both decapitated. Charlotte Corday suffered the same fate, and was publicly declared to be an insult to womanhood. Anne Theroigne, who had led the Parisian women out in the streets to demand bread, was beaten so badly by a mob that she finished her life in an asylum. English women, who acted somewhat more patiently, eventually got the vote before French women. So it may be thought that Astell and More were right to preach patience against revolution.

But if English women did eventually get the vote before French women, it was thanks, if not to Wollstonecraft herself, to women, and men, who defended them by appealing to the same arguments to which Wollstonecraft herself appealed. Nineteenth- and early twentieth-century feminists owed much to Wollstonecraft, whether or not they referred to her directly. Mill's arguments in *The Subjection of Women*, and those of Frances Power Cobbe, are in many ways reiterations of the main points of *A Vindication*. If they do not refer to her directly (perhaps the appalling reputation she acquired shortly after her death made it difficult for respectable Victorian writers to name her), they had almost certainly read her work. The American feminist Amy Goldman had no such qualms, and talked openly of her admiration for Wollstonecraft and the influence her work had exerted on her own thoughts.[7] The revolution, together with the change in values of the nineteenth century, created a backlash against feminism. Obviously, this backlash was felt less outside France, so it makes perfect sense that England should have achieved more earlier, and these achievements have nothing to do with patience, or English women's willingness to accept their lot.

TODAY'S FEMINISTS AND WOLLSTONECRAFT

In her Animadversions, as well as in other chapters, Wollstonecraft makes it clear that she does not think women are different from men in a way that is relevant to their rights. What matters is reason, and that, she insists, is never gendered. Nor is the way in which we use reason. Macaulay does not have a 'masculine intellect', Wollstonecraft says, because there is no such thing. Reason is divine, and all human beings, men or women, partake in it and need to develop it in order to achieve excellence, that is, virtue. So virtue too, she says, is non-gendered. There are no male and female virtues: such relative virtues would be 'inefficacious'. But some of her critics, including Barbauld, think that Wollstonecraft is missing something important: there are differences between men and women, and we need to understand and accept these differences if we are to devise a code of conduct that enables both men and women to become virtuous.

In the late 1970s, the idea that difference matters was taken up again by feminist thinkers (including Julia Kristeva, Luce Irigaray, Hélène Cixous) who argued that sexual differences should not be erased from the law. The law itself was seen as phallocentric, a male instrument, blind to women's needs. So, for example, while a radical feminist might argue that pregnancy and childcare should be treated just like any other disability and granted leave accordingly, difference feminists claim that this is a mistake. Pregnancy is not a disability, but a fundamental part of what it means to be a woman. This and other aspects of womanhood need to be recognized, accepted and legislated for specifically. The law must stop being male-centred under the pretence of being universal, and must become male/female-centred instead.

Difference feminism is at source an essentialist position, one that postulates that men and women have different natures. Wollstonecraft could not possibly have agreed with this view. For her, human beings are essentially rational beings, and reason simply has to be un-gendered. Also, she believes that most of what her contemporaries called feminine qualities were in fact the product of an educational process that assumed and encouraged difference. In some respects, it is less clear whether Wollstonecraft did not in fact believe there were certain essential differences. She claims, for instance, that men are physically stronger than women, so by nature are better at certain things (though she does not say which, and one suspects that she is mostly trying to pacify bruised male egos). She also writes of the woman as mother, a woman's duty to spend time and effort on her children, and in her letter to Talleyrand she deplores the fact that without a proper education, women will not 'spend that time in their nursery […] which they choose to spend at their glass' (68). She does also, however, write of a father's duty in the very same sentence, so it is not clear that she believes motherhood is anything more than parenthood for women.

Note also that Wollstonecraft does not appear to have believed that it is a woman's duty to marry and become a mother. Indeed, she recommends against marriage in some cases, and always against early marriages, on the grounds that they prevent a young woman from acquiring some knowledge and experience of the world which, together with time, is necessary for her education to mature properly (Wollstonecraft 1994: 93–94). She also holds that more professions should be open to women so that they are not forced to marry in order to support themselves.[8]

I discuss Wollstonecraft's attitude to motherhood in Chapter Eight of this book, but aside from this sort of wavering, it looks as though Wollstonecraft would in fact be closer to radical feminists, blaming the oppression of women on patriarchal gender relations, than she would to essentialist difference feminists. It is not entirely clear, though, that difference feminism has to be essentialist, and it may be that such a non-essentialist view would provide useful insight into Wollstonecraft's arguments. So let us look at one now.

One famous application of difference feminism came with Carol Gilligan's response to Kohlberg's research on moral development (Kohlberg 1981; Gilligan 1982). Kohlberg, following Piaget's model of cognitive development, had conducted experiments on people's responses to moral questions. Kohlberg described six stages of development, from egocentrism and relativism to more altruistic, contractual and principle-led moral thinking. Children start off caring only for themselves, and end up as adults either as utilitarians or Kantians, depending on how much they have evolved. This means they will form moral judgments or make moral decisions on the basis of rules that they perceive as applying to all: either rules dictated by the general principle that happiness is the greatest good, or, if they are Kantians, rules derived from reason and the principle of universality. Kohlberg's controversial and disputed finding is this: as subjects matured, he believed their responses were likely to be utilitarian and, in the case of highly mature individuals, Kantian. But before they reached that stage, they would be relativists, placing more importance on the relationships involved in the case than the abstract principles. Kohlberg found that men tended to develop further than women. Men could become Kantian, but women would be relativists or, at best, utilitarians. Many objections have been raised about Kohlberg, ranging from the reliability of his experiments to his claim that Kantian ethics were philosophically superior to utilitarianism. But the most interesting objection came from Gilligan, and addressed the question of whether women were morally less developed than men.

Kohlberg claimed that Kantian morality came closest to the truth because it was what those who reached the highest stage of development chose as their guide. Utilitarianism and relativism were therefore philosophically inferior. Gilligan questioned this. Women, she says, tend to register as either relativists or utilitarians in Kohlberg's tests. In fact they are neither. What Kohlberg interpreted as the tendency to be happiness maximizers was in fact the moral imperative to care for others, a deep concern that one is responsible for the wellbeing of others. What he saw as relativism was in fact a reluctance to apply universal rules to particular situations due to a recognition of their intricacies and uniqueness (Gilligan 1982: 101). So, instead of saying that Kohlberg is wrong, that his experiments portray false differences between men and women, Gilligan prefers to say that women simply speak in a different voice. There are different ways of being moral, different emphases, and women typically prefer to be caring and men impartial.

Gilligan's findings provide a clear example of what difference feminism can achieve. First, a recognition that women sometimes operate in different spheres of society and, as a result, will have different responses to situations and problems. A woman who spends most of her life caring for others will tend to include consideration of those others in her moral deliberations. Gilligan points out that people who think that way have simply been excluded from

Kohlberg's and other psychologists' tests. They have not been accounted for. Second, what follows quite naturally from pointing out that women's reactions are absent from the relevant research is a re-evaluation of the findings. If what seemed like relativism is in fact an instance of caring for others, and is how a lot of women happen to think, then Kohlberg is wrong, both in his description of this developmental stage and in his classification. Thinking like a woman is not an inferior way of being moral, and it certainly is not the same as being a relativist.

However, in recent work, Gilligan (1997) has started to argue, following studies of the moral development of men, that at least for some men what Kohlberg calls relativism may also be best, but that society tends to stifle men's caring impulses. Gilligan, it turns out, does not so much argue for difference as challenge received ideas about what it is to be human and what it is to be male, when these ideas are merged. Wollstonecraft, when she denies that reason is male, is doing the very same thing. To be rational, is not, she says, to be masculine. A woman is just as rational as a man, but does not need to act like one in every respect.

Even though Wollstonecraft may believe that sometimes sexual differences are significant, especially as far as parenthood is concerned, she does not, however, believe that any difference should transpire at the level of education. What does transpire in education, though, is that certain virtues traditionally connected with being females would, Wollstonecraft says, greatly benefit boys. So in her chapter on schooling, she argues that children, boys and girls, should live at home and attend day schools, because that will teach them the kind of virtues one can only learn by living with one's family, in a loving household. This, she hopes, will counteract the libertine ways that boys develop at school, and encourage men to embrace chastity (218), in exactly the same way as she hopes women will.

Thus it seems as though Wollstonecraft recognizes that patriarchal institutions have created a gender divide. But she does not believe the solution is for women to stop being women and become more like men – at least not entirely. She believes they should strive to be human beings, citizens, and that this is something that men should do as well as women. She even believes that men should seek to develop traditionally female virtues such as chastity and gentleness (but not, of course, sensibility). So she would not be entirely against a kind of non-essentialist difference feminism.

One branch of radical feminism that takes into account differences brought about by patriarchal society is MacKinnon's and Dworkin's dominance feminism, arguing that feminine characteristics are created and then devalued by patriarchal institutions. Wollstonecraft, although she goes along with a lot of the devaluation, would nonetheless express some sympathy with this view, I think. Women, she says, are brought to be creatures that will satisfy men's lust, at the cost of their true rational nature and of their health. But at the same time, it is because they think women more sensual and less rational that men deny them a say in how to live their own lives. So, clearly, Wollstonecraft does agree that patriarchal society both creates then devalues feminine attributes. What she would not agree with is that what must be done next is to reassign some value to femininity, respect it as a valid way to live a human life. Instead, she believes strongly that women must be re-educated so that they can be more rational, healthier and less prey to their senses.

It is difficult not to sympathize with Wollstonecraft. Women nowadays may be attached to certain aspects of their femininity: being able to give up work to look after young children, wearing make-up and attractive clothes, at the very least. But these instances of femininity are a world apart from eighteenth-century ideas of what a woman should and should not do. In any case, femininity now is not straightforwardly incompatible with being a citizen with full rights. I say not straightforwardly, because one may still argue quite plausibly that the idea that women get to stay at home with young children, rather than men doing so, or instead of children being sent to nurseries, can be blamed at least in part for the inequality of professional achievements between men and women. If childcare was not perceived as a woman's prerogative, or even duty, there would almost certainly be more nurseries and more women in high positions.

One can see why Wollstonecraft may reject femininity even today for the above reasons. On the other hand, one can also understand how, to women who care about any aspects of their femininity, such zealousness as Wollstonecraft displays in her condemnation would not only be difficult to come to terms with, but also almost certainly insulting. What Wollstonecraft does not seem to perceive is that, if women have come to see themselves as different by nature through a bad system of education, they might nonetheless have created an identity for themselves and thus feel personally under attack when Wollstonecraft tells them they should be otherwise. This is still the case. No woman wants to be told that she is demeaning herself or the human race by acting in ways that she finds natural. So even if, like Wollstonecraft, we are not prepared to say that those feminine qualities created by patriarchal institutions should be recognized as valuable, those women (and men) who have these qualities should be recognized as valuable, and not insulted.

7

TASTE AND UNCLOUDED REASON

VIRTUE AND ETIQUETTE

Chapters Six to Eight of *A Vindication of the Rights of Woman* deal with the various ways in which social mores and customs interfere with the proper moral and intellectual development of women. Because of this, it makes sense to discuss them together. In her Chapter Six, Wollstonecraft writes of the role of early education in failing to produce virtuous individuals, and the inculcation of frivolous manners, which 'enervates' women and turns them into dependent, pleasure-seeking individuals incapable of forming true and lasting relationships. This chapter gives us an interesting insight into Wollstonecraft's take on the role of manners and etiquette in virtuous life, a theme that is taken up again in Chapter Eight, where she discusses the concept of a good reputation. Her views on the matter are subtle. On one hand, she is painfully aware of how manners have in some way replaced virtue in polite society, especially where women are concerned, as they are required for women to keep up the appearance of virtue without being given the means of understanding its true nature. On the other hand, Wollstonecraft tells us that good manners reflect our respect for our fellow human beings, and as such should not be neglected. I draw parallels between what she says on the topic of manners and the writings of her near contemporary Jane Austen, linking both to some more recent writing on that topic. In Chapter Seven, Wollstonecraft discusses the virtues of modesty and chastity: she asks us to distinguish between the real virtues and the mere appearances that women are encouraged to keep up. This leads her, towards the end of that chapter and in most of Chapter Eight, to the question of how a concern for reputation has become more important than a concern for a genuine virtuous character. Again, she tackles the idea of reputation with great subtlety, addressing not only the artificial character of the demands made on women by society, but also the very real harm that can come to a woman who has 'lost' her reputation.

A QUESTION OF MANNERS

Do manners matter, or are they merely superficial markers of class distinction? Wollstonecraft's message on this topic is certainly mixed. On one hand, she pities women who 'are only taught to observe behaviour, and acquire manners rather than morals' (Wollstonecraft 1999/1792: 193); on the other she tells us that good manners are a sign that we 'cherish such an habitual respect for mankind as may prevent us from disgusting a fellow creature for the sake of a present indulgence' (217).

This is a confusing attitude, and we might feel that the second part of it in particular, the regard for manners, has no resonance in current takes on manners. We may feel that as long as we say 'please' and 'thank you', we don't really need to concern ourselves with questions of etiquette, and certainly we think we shouldn't let ourselves be oppressed by them, as eighteenth-century women were. But I think this would be a misrepresentation of contemporary attitudes to manners. Manners still matter to many people, sometimes overtly, sometimes not, and this is not always a sign that we are being oppressed. One indication of this is the (perhaps exaggerated) attention paid to advisers in manner, such as columnist Judith Martin:

> During a White House ceremony in November 2005, Judith Martin was awarded the nation's highest honor in the humanities, the National Humanities Medal, in recognition of her contributions to society as America's foremost etiquette columnist and author. Given by the President of the United States under the auspices of the National Endowment for the Humanities, the Medal honors individuals or groups whose work has deepened the nation's appreciation of the humanities, broadened our citizens' engagement with the humanities, or helped preserve and expand Americans' access to important resources in the humanities.
>
> (www.missmanners.com/home/about-miss-manners.html)

Judith Martin, aka Miss Manners, is a journalist who makes it her business to offer advice on etiquette in newspaper columns as well as on her website. She does not limit herself to the rules of etiquette – anyone can find a book and look these up – but concerns herself mostly with questions of human interaction. What do I do when my neighbour's children come to my house at Halloween to get candy and don't say thank you? Put up with it, Miss Manner says, because Halloween is really not the right time to go around lecturing other people's children. From being something you use to punish children, manners become a way of interacting with them in a more humane and pleasant manner. Karen Stohr, writing on the topic of manners, says that for Judith Martin, 'genuinely good manners preclude the use of etiquette in the service of immoral ends. On this view, using the rules of etiquette to express scorn, disdain, or disapproval towards innocent parties itself constitutes a violation of etiquette' (Stohr 2006: 192).

Stohr asks us to distinguish between genuine and superficial good manners. It is true that superficial good manners often hide a bad intention, that manners are a way in which rich people set themselves apart from the poor. So-called good manners are often a way of making somebody feel bad about themselves, their education, their family background. Pointing out to a dinner guest that they are using the wrong cutlery, or otherwise breaching a rule of etiquette, or even making it obvious to them that they are doing so without actually saying anything, is just offensive, and, Miss Manners tells us, because it is inconsiderate, it is also bad manners. Being superlatively polite to somebody you despise and then make fun of is also not good manners, because it goes hand-in-hand with a fundamental disrespect and dishonesty. It is better manners, probably, to be minimally polite to somebody one dislikes, and then to refrain from talking about them behind their back. We are then offering the minimum of respect that is due to one's fellow beings, making some allowance for prejudice (we might be wrong about the reason why we dislike them), but showing no particular respect or affection, and no wish to become better acquainted.

On the other hand, no-one likes a boor, somebody who is either deliberately offensive or doesn't take the trouble to figure out a way of being that is not offensive. We tolerate a small child who doesn't say 'thank you' at Halloween, but we'd be hurt or offended by an older child who took a gift from us with no acknowledgement, even if we know they are indeed grateful. We expect people to acquire a modicum of good manners, we believe that by saying 'please' and 'thank you' they are showing that they respect us, acknowledging that we matter, that we are part of the same world as them. Being rude to somebody can be perceived by that person as if they were being ignored, as if their presence simply didn't matter. Somebody who doesn't give thanks is often supposed to be selfish and uncaring.

So there appear to be two extremes of behaviour that we dislike – manners without principle, superficial forms of behaviour that hide a lack of concern and respect for one's fellow human beings; and the complete absence of manners, which may or may not hide an absence of principle, but is certainly perceived as such. These are the two vices that Wollstonecraft discusses in her Chapters Six and Eight. And this is the reason why her message is mixed. She does not first dismiss, then praise manners, but she sees that a person may fail to have good manners in two opposite ways. And when a character trait is best understood as a mean between two extremes, our first port of call should, of course, be virtue.

Karen Stohr, in the article in which she discusses Judith Martin, argues that 'the capacity to behave appropriately in social settings is properly understood as a virtue. Genuinely good manners contribute to, and are expressive of, morally important ends, the ends to which someone with full Aristotelian virtue is committed' (Stohr 2006: 189). To say 'thank you' when you receive a gift is to acknowledge that you know the giver has gone to some trouble to please you, perhaps because they want to show their affection, or respect, or gratitude, and that their attempt to do so was at least partly effective. You are pleased, made aware of their affection, respect or gratitude. You are able to understand the nature and value of the sentiment that led them to act, and you want them to know it.

Put this way, good manners do sound as though they might qualify for the title of virtue. Good manners, as understood by Miss Manners, will help make somebody feel comfortable about their own lack of knowledge of the rules of etiquette: they will go hand-in-hand with a desire to be kind, as well as to educate. There is certainly nothing objectionable about manners of that sort; on the contrary, one would be inclined to think they are praiseworthy. It is also true that they go hand-in-hand with the ability to note the detail of our surroundings, figuring out the reason for someone's behaviour, whether lack of manners or intentionally hurtful, finding a way of helping the person modify this behaviour without hurting their feelings and making them feel inferior, and adjusting our own behaviour accordingly, as Elizabeth I reputedly did when she drank the water from her finger bowl so as not to show up a guest who was ignorant of its purpose.

But isn't there still something a little superficial, and especially exclusive, about insisting on manners as the best way of expressing one's virtue? Is it really a kindness to force a child from a disadvantaged background to learn manners, so that they fit in better with rich people and do not show themselves up? Is it really to the advantage of the child, who might be better occupied focusing on acquiring skills that will take him or her out of this disadvantaged background without looking down on his or her own family? Isn't it rather to the advantage of the rich who interact with that child, the rich for whom a lack of etiquette is distasteful, grating? This is certainly not what Stohr has in mind. Good manners are not always a mark of social class. Ovid's tale of Baucis and

Philemon illustrates this: Zeus and Hermes come to a village disguised as poor travellers and ask for hospitality (*Metamorphoses* VIII). Baucis and Philemon welcome them to their rustic cottage, when all their rich neighbours turn them down rudely and bolt their doors. What this illustrates is that truly good manners are not often found in the very rich, who only use them when it appears to be in their interest to do so.

Another consideration is that manners, as they presuppose the ability to acquire a fine understanding of social interactions, are not accessible to all. Anyone on the autism spectrum, for example, will find it extremely difficult to read social cues and respond accordingly, simply because this is a feature of their condition. But would we want to say that people with autism are less virtuous because they find it difficult to learn manners? I think not. We would certainly, in that case, think that manners are a superficial, if useful accomplishment that in no way reflects on these people's good or bad character. In fact, the emphasis on the importance of good manners may go some way towards alienating these people, who are not naturally good at developing good manners, but do not lack respect or affection for their fellow human beings.

A FONDNESS FOR REDCOATS

Those of us who read Helen Fielding's *Bridget Jones's Diary*, or saw the film of the book, may remember how Bridget's mother tells her that unless she says 'pardon' instead of 'what' she'll never find a husband. It seems that Wollstonecraft is of a similar opinion, in that she believes that women of better manners are more likely to be satisfied in their love lives. But for her, this goes hand-in-hand with education, in that women whose feelings are heightened at the cost of their reason will make 'rakes' of them, superficial beings who naturally turn to those like them. So, Wollstonecraft says, it is natural that these women should turn to fun-loving officers for love: 'a passion for a scarlet coat is so natural that it never surprised me' (193).

If Jane Austen read Wollstonecraft, which, although not documented, given the popularity of Wollstonecraft's books at the time is highly likely, she probably had this passage in mind when she wrote the characters of Lydia and Kitty Bennet in *Pride and Prejudice*. Unlike their older sisters Jane and Elizabeth, whose father took care that they should be educated, and unlike their sister Mary, a natural bookworm, Lydia and Kitty did not benefit from much teaching or reading. They are 'silly' girls, whose main purpose in life is to wear nice clothes, go to parties and gossip. So when the Bennet girls walk into town and meet some officers, Lydia and Kitty immediately begin to flirt. The officers are 'charming', they have 'easy manners'. When, at home, they recount their adventure to their parents, Mr Bennet scolds and calls them silly, but Mrs Bennet recalls how she too used to be 'fond of a red coat'. Of course their liking of officers ends badly: Lydia runs away with Mr Wickham and is hereafter 'ruined', so has to marry him. The message is clear: easy manners without morals is a recipe for disaster.

So it is not surprising that Wollstonecraft appears to believe that happiness in love is linked to a strong education: 'Were women more rationally educated, could they take a more comprehensive view of things, they would be contented to love but once in their lives' (195). Obviously this is overstated, if it means that educated women will not fall in love more than once. Wollstonecraft herself did. But at least in both cases where her feelings were reciprocated and she developed a relationship with the other person, she would have been contented to stay with that person for the rest of her life – had that been possible. She did not look over her shoulder to see if someone more attractive came along. She did not fall under the influence of another's charms to the extent that it endangered her relationships. What Wollstonecraft could be taken to mean, if we want to be charitable, is that an educated woman is more likely to want her love and relationship to grow together, and to have a certain amount of success in achieving this. Again, for the sake of charity, she is not saying that a woman who has worked all her life and has not so much as been taught to read properly will be an inconsequential flirt – she is talking of those women who could have been educated, given their social class, but were not, and instead were taught to become women of 'sensibility' or frivolous gossips. She is talking of middle-class women whose education was neglected because no-one cared to teach them, like Elizabeth's younger sisters in *Pride and Prejudice*, who were simply unlucky that their father got bored with teaching girls before their turn came.

Let us take another example from Austen, *Mansfield Park*, in which Fanny Price comes to live with her rich cousins the Bertrams. Fanny's cousins Maria and Julia are given a governess who is paid to teach them what is supposed to matter for young women, a bit of this, a bit of that, some drawing, some French, singing, and manners, deportment, dress. Fanny, whose education is perceived to matter less – she is only a poor relative and will not make a good marriage – picks up what she can from their old books, but mostly is guided in her readings by Edmund, her kind older cousin, until she eventually becomes his intellectual equal. All the Bertram children have good manners, but only Edmund's are genuine, only he would always refrain from doing or saying something that would hurt somebody else. As the 'inferior' in the household, Fanny is often hurt by all except Edmund, despite their good manners.

When the cousins are grown up, an attractive new neighbour, Miss Crawford, comes into the story. Miss Crawford plays the harp beautifully, but her education at the hands of a drunk and rude marine officer and his bitter wife has been very patchy. Edmund's affections waver between her and Fanny. He falls under Miss Crawford's charm early on, and tries to disregard the obvious defects of her character, which he attributes to her poor education, until she shows herself in such a bad light that he has to give up on her. Then, rather implausibly perhaps, he starts to return Fanny's affections. The expensively but superficially educated sisters, Maria and Julia, suffer much the same fate as Lydia and Kitty in *Pride and Prejudice*, if worse, because they are older and richer, so their fall is from a greater height. Both are in love with Mr Crawford, Miss Crawford's amoral but very attractive brother, and they fight over him, losing each other's friendship in the process. The older one marries out of spite someone she does not love, and then elopes with Mr Crawford. She is banished to the colonies; her sister, guilty of less, but with similar inclinations, is put under close surveillance by her father.

Austen writes beautifully about what happens to women who are not well educated, and she is wise enough to see that, even in rich families, it is a matter of luck whether or not a woman is offered a decent education. Indeed, on her accounts not many men are properly educated either – apart from those intended for the clergy, and those who actually desire to be educated, many of the men in her novels are inconsequential fops, or slightly dangerous adventurers whose intellectual and moral limits mean that they'll be trouble – and they usually are. Her observations, in the form of literary portraits, chime in very well with Wollstonecraft's theories. Both believe that the ability to love the right person, and to form a lasting relationship with that person, is linked to a decent education, and both believe that the acquisition of superficial manners, such as are seen in many of their contemporaries, is likely to interfere with this ability.

A GOOD REPUTATION

Both Lydia Bennet and Maria Bertram lose their reputation when they give in to their desires. It seems that a good reputation is intrinsically linked to manners, in that it is gained or obtained on the strength of what society thinks of us. It is certainly linked with appearance, the '*Qu'en dira-t'on*' – 'what will people say' effect. A reputation, like good manners, is what helps us maintain our place in society. In the final few pages of her Chapter Seven, but mostly in Chapter Eight, Wollstonecraft discusses the pernicious effects of the importance placed on reputation. Her discussion is clearly linked to her thoughts on the virtues of chastity and modesty in the first half of Chapter Seven. Thus, when she brings up the idea of a good reputation in Chapter Seven, it is as a contrast to real chastity:

> I doubt whether chastity will produce modesty, though it may propriety of conduct, when it is merely a respect for the opinion of the world, and when coquetry and the love-lorn tales of novelists employ the thoughts. Nay, from experience and reason, I should be led to expect to meet with more modesty amongst men than women, simply because men exercise their understanding more than women.

(202)

Where chastity is simply acting the part society expects us to act, it will not lead to modesty, presumably because it is not a virtue. It may be rehearsed as a virtue – it may be the product of habituation, but what is missing, Wollstonecraft tells us, is reason's part in the creation of the virtue, the conscious reflection on what constitutes virtuous behaviour and what does not, which must follow the process of habituation for a character trait to become a virtue.

Despite this, Wollstonecraft tells us that this superficial kind of chastity is what educationalists such as Rousseau and Gregory encourage in women, and she gives us to understand that their view reflects, on the whole, the popular one. Women should not be reflexive, yet they must behave in the right way – appearances are everything. The ambivalence we detected in Rousseau in Chapter Six is again at play here: women need be virtuous, but they are, after all, prey to their senses and incapable of reason. So even if they are educated to be chaste, there is only so much that can be achieved with such fickle creatures. Hence they must also be taught to protect their reputation.

The theme continues in Wollstonecraft's next chapter, which begins by noting that the drive to acquire and maintain a good reputation is not a virtue, but merely a way to ensure that one keeps one's place in the world (210). This concern for reputation is forced on women, she says, and destroys not only their morality, but their ability to think critically:

> for the practised dissembler at last, become the dupe to his own arts, loses that sagacity, which has been justly termed common sense; namely a quick perception of common truths: which are constantly received as such by the unsophisticated mind, though it might not have had sufficient energy to discover them itself, when obscured by local prejudices.
>
> (210)

In other words, the concern for a good reputation damages the mind, encourages petty thinking, and discourages attempts at reasoning about the larger picture and honesty about one's motives. This is maybe why Rousseau, who did not think much of women's intellectual abilities in the first place, felt that reputation was so important for women 'no less indispensable than chastity', as he put it. Whereas men should depend on their own good judgment of themselves, their conscience as it were, women owe it to their potential husband to be seen to be good, and should be educated with this aim in mind – not that they should be good, but that they should know how to appear to be good (212). What Wollstonecraft argues is that rather than being considered of equal importance to chastity, a good reputation in fact carries all the weight, and it is considered better to have a good reputation and not be chaste than to be chaste without the reputation. Thus the famous conundrum proposed to Socrates by Plato's brothers in Book II of the *Republic*: is it better to be virtuous but to be thought not to be and be treated accordingly, or to lack in virtue but to have a sterling reputation and be a social success? Socrates chooses the former, and argues that it is always better to be virtuous. It seems as if Rousseau and others might say that men should agree with Socrates – but that women should take the other option.

One reason why a woman should maintain her reputation over her virtue may well be that she is not deemed capable of proper virtue anyway. If virtue requires reason, and women are less reasonable and more instinctual then men, as Rousseau believes, then they will not excel at virtue. Reputation will at least preserve the appearance of virtue, and save husbands and fathers from being challenged directly about the behaviour of their wives and daughters, so it may be as much as we can expect from women.

A kinder argument, maybe one that Dr Gregory would put forward, is this. Women are not in a position, in eighteenth-century society, either to choose their own husband or to make an independent life for themselves. Therefore their happiness, or at least their comfort, depends on being chosen by a man and staying in his good graces. But a man also has a place to maintain in society, and that place depends in part on society's perception of his wife. So a man will not choose a wife who has a poor reputation, even if he knows that that reputation is unfounded. He will not be kind to a wife who has lost her reputation, as that will reflect badly on him.

Wollstonecraft does not deny that reputation matters at all, and she understands that, in any kind of society, it matters to both men and women to some extent to have a good reputation. But what she does not believe is that preserving a reputation requires very much over and beyond acting in a way that is deserving of a good reputation, that is, being virtuous. In this she follows Adam Smith, who believed that a deservedly good reputation will generally look after itself. She quotes Smith discussing a case very much like that put to Socrates in the *Republic*: a virtuous man acquires a bad reputation through bad luck. But, Smith (quoted by Wollstonecraft) says,

> Accidents of this kind, however, are perhaps still more rare, and still more contrary to the common course of things than those of the second [people losing everything to a natural catastrophe]; and it still remains true that the practice of truth, justice, and humanity, is a certain and almost infallible method of acquiring what those virtues chiefly aim at, the confidence and love of those we live with.
>
> (213)

Almost infallible, Smith tells us: but this is probably not good enough for the young woman who finds herself cheated out of a good marriage because her enemies have placed her in a compromising position and thereby ruined her reputation. But this kind of situation, Wollstonecraft argues, is very melodramatic: it may happen in *Les Liaisons Dangereuses* or *Camille*, but not usually in real life. Or, if it does, it is an exception to the norm and therefore not something we should use as a constant guideline or warning. An eighteenth-century parent may well object that, although rare and unusual, this kind of accidental or spiteful ruining of a perfectly well behaved girl's reputation is such a tragedy that we must always look out for it. But there is a difference between something being rare and unusual, and something happening mostly in novels. Not that it's only in novels that people are cruel and will try to harm someone's reputation, but it tends to be the case that only in novels are they really successful. Wollstonecraft and Smith believe that, at the end of the day, virtue will out. This is not just some naïve sort of optimism, but a deep understanding of what virtue means. We do not attribute virtue or vice to somebody we care about merely on the basis of having witnessed one piece of behaviour – we look at a person's entire lifestyle, at choices they've made over the years, relationships they've established, etc.

If the piece of behaviour that is causing people to frown is 'out of character', then it is unlikely to be taken very seriously. People will at least wonder if there might have been a set-up.

This sounds plausible. Certainly, we would not suddenly distrust our wife or husband because one day they came home with lipstick on their shirt collar. We might be suspicious, review past incidents and observe their subsequent behaviour. But we would not condemn them outright as guilty of infidelity unless we already thought they were capable of it. This is because the person whose reputation is at risk is somebody we know, someone who's character we've observed over the years, and we do not give up our good opinion of these people on such flimsy evidence.

On the other hand, when a girl's reputation is ruined, it is not ruined with her family, or the man she hopes to marry – it is ruined with society at large. If a girl is caught in a compromising position, her husband-to-be may well trust that she was not at fault. But he might no longer feel he is in a position to marry her and have children by her. To do so may well result in his losing his place in society and not being able to provide for his wife and future children. So the fact that when you know someone, you are not willing to question their virtue lightly, does not affect the dangers of a lost reputation unless it is also the case that people at large do not judge without good evidence.

Unfortunately, that is not the case. People do judge on very poor evidence, we do attribute virtues and vices without having the slightest knowledge of a person's character. This is what social psychologists have called the fundamental attribution error. We have a tendency to want to explain others' behaviour by attributing personality traits we have not really observed. One reason why we do this is that we hold a 'just world hypothesis' – we assume that people tend to get what they deserve, that there is 'no smoke without fire', and that ultimately, if someone is being treated badly, they must have done something to deserve it. However interesting, these theories are far from being infallible – the very tests designed to prove them were inconclusive. Yet it is hard to deny that society works this way, that gossip will harm a person's prospects, and that people will assume the worst even in the absence of reasonable evidence (Jones and Harris 1967).

I think Wollstonecraft is fully aware of this, and neither she nor Smith argues that bad reputations will not be created out of nowhere, and that lives will not be ruined by spiteful gossip. But both are describing what they take to be the power of reputation in sensible society: not a society that is ruled by idle gossipers, but in which most people will at least attempt to look at the evidence of a person's character before deciding it has been ruined. In this context, I think, away from the world of Choderlos de Laclos' *Les Liaisons Dangereuses*, they are right. A reputation is hard to ruin, and therefore should not be the main concern behind our actions.

TASTE: MORAL AND AESTHETIC VIRTUES

Towards the end of her Chapter Eight, Wollstonecraft draws a link between the virtues of chastity and modesty on the one hand, and 'taste' (as in 'good or bad taste') on the other. There is nothing terribly unusual there. Eighteenth-century writers commonly used the word 'taste' to refer to either moral or aesthetic qualities. In *Of the Standard of Taste*, Hume describes the good critic as someone who possesses 'strong sense, united to delicate sentiment, improved by practice, perfected by comparison, and cleared of all prejudice' (Hume 2007: 247). If one read this out of context, one would be hard pressed indeed to decide whether Hume was talking about morality or aesthetics. Also, there are strong parallels in his treatments of moral and aesthetic judgements. He defines both in terms of sentiments, feelings of approbation that are not directly caused by 'something in the object', but not entirely subjective either.

Notwithstanding eighteenth-century practices, Wollstonecraft's transition from morality to taste is abrupt and strange. One minute she is discussing male chastity and the relation of chastity to other virtues which make or break a character. The very next paragraph finds her rather harshly criticizing French women who eat (or drink) to excess and dare to talk of their resulting indigestion, or those who stay up so outrageously late that they cannot be sensible the next day. What, one wants to say, has any of this to do with chastity, or with virtue? How can a propensity to mention that one's stomach feels a bit funny raise anything like the same level of moral outrage as a the rape of a young woman by a libertine? Is an indigestion really a 'brutal excess'? One senses that Wollstonecraft has moved rather too swiftly from expressing what she regards, rightly, as a universal sentiment, to something rather more personal: she finds this sort of behaviour distasteful.

But Wollstonecraft's rationale for linking taste and morality does in fact encompass both types of violation. She writes that 'Nature must ever be the standard of taste, the gauge of appetite' (217). Anything that nature does not dictate must therefore be excessive. Nature does not dictate that we overeat, nor does it dictate that women should spend their time looking pretty to the detriment of their health and the wellbeing of the children, just so they can attract men whose taste are increasingly 'fastidious'. What is by nature's standard excessive, Wollstonecraft argues, is for us disgusting. Our taste is formed by nature in the first place, and therefore we should not go against it if we want to please. She derives a moral rule from this: 'simply to cherish such an habitual respect for mankind as may prevent us from disgusting a fellow creature for the sake of a present indulgence' (217). Thus the rule for living a virtuous life applies equally well to table manners – do not act in such a way as to offend others' taste. Let nature moderate your choices, do not fall into excess merely because it is fashionable. All very true – but one wonders how Wollstonecraft reconciles these views with the claim that chastity is a virtue. Does nature really ask us to refrain from sexual intercourse until we are married? Well, no. And it is fairly clear from her behaviour, if nothing else, that Wollstonecraft did not believe this either. But what she does believe is that chastity is a virtue, hence that there are two vices of extreme, abstinence obviously being one of them. So she might well believe that having more than one sexual partner, or having a partner with whom one is not seriously emotionally engaged, is unchaste. This would be less obviously flaunting of nature: after all, some animals are monogamous. But it's not entirely clear that it would be against nature not to be chaste in that sense either.

Wollstonecraft takes up again the discussion of moral and aesthetic taste in her Chapter Twelve:

A taste for the fine arts requires great cultivation; but not more than a taste for the virtuous affections; and both suppose that enlargement of mind which opens so many sources of mental pleasure. Why do people hurry to noisy scenes, and crowded circles? I should answer, because they want activity of mind, because they have not cherished the virtues of the heart. They only, therefore, see and feel in the gross, and continually pine after variety, finding every thing that is simple insipid.

(250–51)

She goes on to argue that a woman who is overly fond of pleasure does not enter into the 'minutiae of domestic taste' because she lacks judgment, 'the foundation of all taste'. Such a woman will be just as likely, she says, to prefer a gross caricature over a fine landscape, and to enjoy spending time with her lapdog rather than her own children. In other words, to be lacking in taste in one area almost certainly means that one is lacking in judgment, and therefore taste, in other areas. This is, of course, controversial. We all know people whose behaviour is saintly, and yet who do not have even an inkling of taste as far as beauty is concerned. These people may wear terrible clothes, they may have a deaf ear as far as music is concerned, enjoy a child's picture as much as a masterpiece. But none of these traits needs be the result of a true lack of taste. They may be the result of a physiological incapacity – being tone deaf, or colour blind. They may be due to a lack of exposure: someone who has not benefited from an artistic education will not care for a masterpiece. But this is not a lack of taste in the same way as preferring a crude caricature over a beautiful landscape – it is, rather, unrealized taste.

We have all heard of these evil masterminds whose taste in art is impeccable. There are the sadist collectors, the criminals who cry when listening to a violin concerto. It is not clear to me that these cases do in fact represent an objection to Wollstonecraft. She says that aesthetic and moral taste are linked, and that in the absence of one, we may well suspect the absence of the other, or at least not be surprised at it. She does not say that it is a necessary or a sufficient condition of moral virtue that one should also have taste. Just as a saintly old woman can know nothing about music because she is tone deaf, or because she has never been taught how to listen, great collectors of art may lack moral virtue because they are sociopaths, or because they were brought up in such a way that it is impossible for them to be virtuous. Wollstonecraft tells us that taste and virtue tend to go together, that they come from the same ultimate source – sound judgment – not that they cannot exist separately.

Even with those qualifications, it remains, nonetheless, that a lot of judgment is being heaped on us all at once, especially on women. We are supposed to have impeccable taste not only as far as our moral judgments are concerned, but regarding domestic arrangements, manners and fine art. And if we fail in one of the latter three, we run the risk of people assuming that we are morally depraved. So if you have a tacky picture in your home, if you feed your children ready-prepared meals, if you wear your heels a bit too high, your skirt a bit too short, if you eat too much chocolate and are overweight, chances are, Wollstonecraft will think you're not terribly virtuous. She is not alone in making these types of judgment – we all have a certain tendency to frown on a man whose personal hygiene is less than ideal, whose office is a mess; or on a woman who does not give her children enough 'home-cooked' food, who does not exercise and 'lets herself go'. Some of these concerns are genuine: we do want people to maintain a certain degree of unoffensiveness in their appearance – as Wollstonecraft says, there is something objectionable about inspiring disgust in one's fellow beings. But this needs to be strongly moderated. Some people find women's unshaven legs disgusting. Some people are offended by a poor haircut, or clothes that are not ironed. Clearly, such details should not lead to moral condemnation.

Perhaps more worryingly, even, we have a long history of taking offence at what differs from the norm. So, for example, homosexuality is still regarded by some as offensive, characterized as disgusting, even. And this disgust that homosexuality supposedly inspires in some people was, for a long time in Europe (and still in some other parts of the world), considered sufficient grounds for moral and legal censure. This is clearly a case where linking 'taste' to morals is highly dangerous and should certainly lead us to question whether people's claim to be disgusted always represents genuine 'taste' of the kind that Hume would recognize, or is just an instance of ignorant prejudice.

What is regarded as distasteful is often very strongly gendered, and women are much more the target of such judgments, it seems, than men, who are just expected to go along as well as they can and seek help from a wife in order to sort out the details of their daily life. Wollstonecraft is no exception to this bias: although she criticizes the lack of chastity in both men and women, she reserves her accusations of tastelessness for women. Granted, it is women's habits and perceptions of their own place in society that she seeks to reform. But this level of criticism of women's habits does make her general argument a little less convincing. However, if we become aware of this failing in her writing, at the same time we realize that we are guilty of the same, so the result is that we are in a position to take up a Wollstonecraft-style argument, but more strongly.

8

RATIONAL FELLOWSHIP OR SLAVISH OBEDIENCE?

LOVE, MARRIAGE AND FAMILY

WOMAN IN SOCIETY

In Chapters Nine to Eleven of *A Vindication of the Rights of Woman*, Wollstonecraft tackles a number of questions surrounding the roles of women in society. She discusses love and marriage, daughterhood, motherhood, but also – significantly – the professions that she feels should be open to women. From the point of view of the modern reader, it has to be good that these chapters come towards the end of the book: aside from the very important claims about women and work, they are a lot less radical, a lot more supportive of the *status quo*, than anything else Wollstonecraft has to say. Had these chapters come first, it is doubtful that Wollstonecraft would have come to be regarded as a revolutionary defender of women's rights. This would be a mistake, as even in these chapters Wollstonecraft develops several important arguments in defence of women's rights, but there are nonetheless passages that could easily offend a modern feminist.

For one thing, in these chapters she seems to believe that motherhood is a natural vocation for women, and that in order to fulfil their roles as citizens, women must assume prime responsibility for the upbringing of their children. This includes breastfeeding. And it means putting one's maternal duties before love for one's husband. A woman should seek her husband's love not by making herself interesting or attractive as a woman, but by showing herself to be a good mother and efficient housewife. None of this sounds particularly like a vindication of women's rights.

At the same time, Wollstonecraft does not believe it is possible for a woman to become a good mother unless she is emancipated, that is, unless she has achieved a degree of independence and autonomy equal to what a male citizen may expect to achieve. Her Chapter Nine, in which she talks of marriage, is also one of the only places in the book where she mentions citizenship for women and women's legal situation with respect to marriage. The arguments she has developed in the previous chapters are brought to bear on her views: a woman can neither be a good wife nor a good mother, she argues, unless she has been well educated and can think for herself.

The views on filial duty and parenthood developed in Chapters Ten and Eleven are more radical than the points she makes relating solely to women's role. She argues that the relationship between parent and child is not sacred to the extent that a child owes their parents unconditional obedience. A child should also think for themself, give respect only where respect is due, and obey only orders that he or she judges to be reasonable. She claims that the duty towards one's parents is 'absurd', thereby putting a lot of pressure on parents who are not, by either nature or education, at ease with reasoning, but still would quite like their children to obey them, at least while they are children.

In the following five sections I consider various strands in these three chapters and try to make some sense of the tension between Wollstonecraft's radical attitudes to parenthood and her still very conventional beliefs about women's roles as wives and mothers. I start with love, then discuss Wollstonecraft's views on the institution of marriage, then on women's various roles once they are married; finally, I discuss good and bad parenting according to Wollstonecraft.

LOVE AND MARRIAGE

Before we discuss the institution of marriage, and the roles women fall into once they are married, it makes sense to ask why, on Wollstonecraft's account, women should get married in the first place. This question can be taken to mean two different things. The first is whether women should get married at all, whether they might not be better off remaining single (at least as far as the law is concerned). The second would ask what a woman's motivations should be in deciding to get married – love, or something else?

First, Wollstonecraft does not believe that women have a duty to get married or have children. She feels that marriage should not be the only choice available for women who do not have money of their own. Instead, she argues, women should be able to enter into professions and support themselves without having to sell themselves to a husband in exchange for a roof over their head. She seems to concur with Daniel Defoe in describing marriage as a kind of legal prostitution (Wollstonecraft 1999/1792: 130). Women, she feels, should not be forced into marriage just so that they may survive or even rise in the world.

Given these views on marriage, one would expect it to follow that Wollstonecraft believes women should marry for love. Yet, at the time of writing *A Vindication*, she did not. She believed that both and men and women should avoid following their passion in choosing a partner. In Chapter Nine of *A Vindication*, she makes it very clear that, as far as she is concerned, what makes a successful marriage is not romantic love or infatuation, but 'well regulated affections; and an affection includes a duty' (222). In a sense, there is nothing particularly outrageous about this. A marriage cannot last on passion alone – it does need lasting feelings for one another, of the kind that encourage respect, understanding and cooperation. In that respect, it helps if both partners are 'pulling their weight' as far as keeping the household going is concerned. Marriages in which this does not happen, in which there is no agreement as to who should do what, and no discussion of feelings about household duties, do tend to go badly. So yes, there are duties involved in being happily married. But there is a difference between saying that a married couple should be aware of and respectful of each other's needs, that they should take their roles as husband and wife seriously, and saying that we shouldn't marry for love. But this is indeed what Wollstonecraft says.

Lest we think we are doing Wollstonecraft an injustice in saying that she rejects the idea of marrying for love, I suggest we go back to earlier chapters. In her Chapter Three, Wollstonecraft draws a comparison between a woman who marries for love and one who marries from affection. The former will not marry well, she says. A woman who 'has learned only to please' will not attract a sensible man, as a sensible man will be thinking of starting a family, not just of romance, and no one sensible, she says, will 'choose to marry a *family* for love'. Such a woman will therefore be unhappy and make others, especially her children, unhappy. As a woman who has been taught to please, rather than think and do her duty, she is unfit to be either a wife or mother, Wollstonecraft tells us. One target of Wollstonecraft's criticism here is clearly Rousseau, who thinks that women should be brought up to be attractive to men, and provide them with rest from a life spent in business or politics. A woman, in Rousseau's view, should therefore know how to look pretty, be amusing, and not tax him with serious conversation. But Wollstonecraft believes that a woman brought up as Rousseau says she should be will not make a good partner and will fail as a parent. Although this is a harsh judgment, and almost certainly an exaggeration, we can see the reasoning behind Wollstonecraft's claims. Knowing only how to please is not attractive in the long run – beauty fades, and people tire of one person's physical attractions. Marriages are more successful when partners can respect each other. Certainly, a parent whose main concern is looks does not make a good parent. One should have no dispute with this.

What is much less clear is why Wollstonecraft thinks that one will marry for love only if one is frivolous and unsuited to the role of wife or parent. Her view is rather extreme. She even goes so far as to claim that a neglected wife will make the best mother (97). There is a distinction here that Wollstonecraft is trying, perhaps unsuccessfully, to draw. In contrast to the 'silly' woman who marries for love, Wollstonecraft draws a picture of a sensible woman, eager to perform her duties as a mother and wife. Such a woman secures her husband's respect before love dies its 'natural death', to be replaced by 'friendship and forbearance' (118). When she is prematurely widowed, she takes care that she does not fall in love again. She 'represses the first faint dawning of natural inclination, before it ripens into love, and in the bloom of life forgets her sex – forgets the pleasure of an awakening passion, which might again have been inspired and returned. [...] Her children have her love and her brightest hopes are beyond the grave, where her imagination often strays' (119).

The wise widow, unlike the silly wife, is in control of her emotional life and she reaps the rewards of her efforts. She has her husband's respect and friendship during his lifetime as well as her children's love, and after she is widowed, she has the comfort of knowing that she can fulfil both her own role and her husband's, that she can manage, and that her children, thanks to her, will flourish. This is what Wollstonecraft wants us to picture: a woman in control of her own life, who knows what she wants and is getting it. This is also very far from what her contemporaries would have expected a successful woman to look like. A woman did well if she married well, with the emphasis on the act of getting married, rather than the marriage itself. As long as one secured a house, a sufficient income, a place in society, maybe even a title, one did well. What happened after-wards was irrelevant. What this means is that the success of the marriage was not really the woman's success, but belonged to her father, who was able to both get rid of a daughter and consolidate his place in society by having his daughter make a good marriage. It is hard to see in what other sense marrying someone without any reason to believe it would lead to long-term happiness would constitute success.

Wollstonecraft wants a woman who marries to be in control of her own life, not the slave to her husband's moods and appetites. But why does she believe this is not compatible with a love match? This might simply be a reflection on her fundamental distrust of what she, and many of her contemporaries, regarded as love. Love, she says, 'regarded as an animal appetite, cannot long feed on itself without expiring. And this extinction in its own flame, may be termed the violent death of love. But the wife who has thus been rendered licentious, will probably endeavour to fill the void left by the loss of her husband's attention' (144).

Love in that sense is not the lasting feeling of belonging that two beings who know each other feel for each other, and that gives them the desire, and often the ability, to build a life, a family together. This kind of love is not what one feels at first sight, but something that grows with acquaintance. It does not preclude love at first sight or physical attraction, but it is something more than that. When people nowadays marry for love, they marry somebody they know, not somebody they have only just met and exchanged a few words with. In Wollstonecraft's time, marrying for love was exactly that: marrying somebody one had a physical attraction to, somebody who called forth romantic feelings, but not somebody one knew at all. The rules of etiquette, which forbade close social interactions between boys and girls, made sure that this was not possible.

So this is it: for Wollstonecraft, the kind of love that newlyweds are likely to feel for each other is like a drug, something that makes them feel good but wears off, leaving them desperate for more and unable to appreciate what they do have. She does not think that romantic or passionate love can have a lasting effect in a relationship once the first fires die down. She does not think it can be revived again and again. Because of this, she recommends that passion should be discouraged in young couples so they can grow to esteem and respect each other. Passion, she feels, would not allow them to do this. It would force them to live in the now, and to see only those aspects of each other that they found particularly alluring.

INDEPENDENCE

In her Chapter Nine, Wollstonecraft tackles the question of women's independence, which she has discussed only indirectly through her emphasis on women's need to be educated in the same way as men, and their equal capacity for virtue. Here she is more direct and specific:

> There must be more equality established in society, or morality will never gain ground, and this virtuous equality will not rest firmly even

when founded on a rock, if one half of mankind be chained to its bottom by fate, for they will be continually undermining it through ignorance or pride.

It is vain to expect virtue from women till they are, in some degree, independent of men; nay, it is vain to expect that strength of natural affection, which would make them good wives and mothers.

(221)

Equality, undermined by the respect paid to property, fails to be established, not only in society as a whole, where 'one class presses on another', but within the family unit – wives are dependent on the husbands who hold the property. Relations are perverted, and the wife, instead of loving her husband as an equal, has nothing to offer but 'spaniel like affection'. That is, if she has any affection at all, and does not simply become 'cunning, mean and selfish', which, it seems, would be a fairly natural reaction to finding oneself entirely dependent on a man chosen for her by her parents. But what is important here is that, whatever vice such a wife is bound to develop, it is not out of spite, not because she finds her situation unbearable and seeks revenge, but because it is simply not possible for a dependent to be virtuous. Virtue requires the exercise of reason. The exercise of reason requires that one learns to think independently. A dependent being does not think independently.

For Wollstonecraft, the worship of property has a negative effect on all those involved. A woman who sees her every desire satisfied through money does not develop the sense that she has any duties to perform. She simply waits for what she regards as her dues to come to her. But, Wollstonecraft tells us, if she does not perform her duties, she cannot be virtuous – virtue comes via the regular exercise of one's duty, not through indolence. The same is true of her husband, who also has to be habituated to performing his duties in order to become virtuous. The real effect of hereditary property on society is therefore the lack of virtue.

I mean, therefore, to infer that the society is not properly organized which does not compel men and women to discharge their respective duties by making it the only way to acquire that countenance from their fellow-creatures, which every human being wishes some way to attain. The respect, consequently which is paid to wealth and personal charms, is a true north-east blast, that blights the tender blossoms of affection and virtue.

(222)

In Chapter Nine, not only does Wollstonecraft demand equality within the family, but she actually refers directly to women's legal situation, for the first and only time in her book.

The laws respecting woman, which I mean to discuss in a future part, make an absurd unit of a man and his wife; and then by the easy transition of considering him as responsible, she is reduced to a mere cipher.

(226)

This sentence does clear up somewhat the mystery of why Wollstonecraft, although her book is ostensibly about rights, never mentions the law. She is clearly intending to discuss that aspect of her thought in a second volume, which she never wrote, but which she alludes to in advertisement. But it also seems that the question of women's legal rights is highly relevant to her discussion in this chapter. Twice she brings up women's citizenship.

But, to render her really virtuous and useful, she must not, if she discharge her civil duties, want, individually, the protection of civil laws; she must not be dependent on her husband's bounty for her subsistence during his life, or support after his death——for how can a being be generous who has nothing of its own? Or virtuous, who is not free?

(227)

This short passage tells us all we need to know regarding Wollstonecraft's attitude to legal rights and citizenship: a woman cannot be virtuous if she is dependent on her husband, either legally or materially. Not only that, Wollstonecraft takes care to emphasize, but she will not be a good wife or mother. A being whose intellect and morality is stunted cannot love as she should.

She can only lavish dog-like affection, but that is neither satisfying to a husband nor nurturing to a child.

Nor does Wollstonecraft stop at the suggestion that women should have rights – she feels they should take an active part in government, that they should be represented.

> I may excite laughter, by dropping a hint, which I mean to pursue, some future time, for I really think that women ought to have representatives, instead of being arbitrarily governed without having any direct share allowed them in the deliberation of government.
>
> (228)

It is interesting that she brings up directly the question of rights only when she is discussing marriage. It is not because she is presenting marriage as the worst violation of women's rights (though, as we saw, she does refer to it in an earlier chapter as legal prostitution). Maybe, rather, she feels that while she argues for ways in which women may be better wives and mothers, she will find a more willing audience for her more 'hardcore' views. She will risk laughter rather than outrage if she presents her ideas in this manner. This may also explain why, in this chapter, so many of the more radical passages end on a very un-radical note, reminding the reader that women are wives and mothers.

A WOMAN'S PLACE

It may be the case that Wollstonecraft emphasises women's feminine duties in order to sweeten the pill of equal rights. But we may feel that she pushes this line a bit far. She makes it a condition of citizenship that a mother should be a good educator: 'The wife, in the present state of things, who is faithful to her husband, and neither suckles nor educates her children, scarcely deserves the name of a wife and has no right to that of a citizen' (227). This is not an isolated point. Just a few paragraphs before, she tells us that 'speaking of woman at large, their first duty is to themselves as rational creatures, and the next, in point of importance, as citizens, is that which includes so many, of a mother' (226). Instead of giving up this train of thought when she moves on to the next chapter, she reinforces her arguments by claiming that 'the care of children in their infancy is one of the grand duties annexed to the female character by nature' (233). This, it seems, goes back on her earlier and often-repeated claim that there were no moral differences between men and women, merely physical ones. So nature has made it impossible for men to breastfeed infants – but why turn this into a matter of character and duty?

Part of the answer to this rather puzzling question is to be found in her Chapter Three, in which Wollstonecraft defends the view that men and women must share the same virtues – that there is no such thing as a feminine virtue:

> Women, I allow, may have different duties to fulfil; but they are human duties, and the principle that should regulate the discharge of them, I sturdily maintain, must be the same.
>
> (119)

But what, one asks, are *human* duties? I suggest that they be contrasted to what she has called elsewhere 'grand duties' – duties that concern our being worthy of the afterlife, divine duties, as it were. Human duties, by contrast, are what one needs to fulfil in order to be a good citizen, in order to make the best one can of this life. This does fit in with the notion (226) that women's first duty is to live as rational beings, and then to be good mothers in order to be good citizens. It does not fit, however, with Wollstonecraft using the term 'grand duty' to refer to the mothering of infants (233). But it may be that she is using the term loosely in that passage. All the other evidence seems to point to a distinction she makes between divine duties, which concern one's reason and which are equal for men and women; and citizens' duties, which differ for men and women without being incompatible with the development of the more important first category of duties.

Thankfully, Wollstonecraft does not limit her discussion of women's place in society to the roles of being a wife and a mother. In fact, she suggests very strongly that, for a woman who does not need to do all the work in her home herself, a woman who can afford servants, it is not enough that she should be a wife and a mother. Society ought to afford her more opportunities to make herself useful. Women, she says, 'might certainly study the art of healing, and be physicians as well as nurses. And midwifery, decency seems to allot to them, though I am afraid the word midwife, in our dictionaries, will soon give place to accoucheur' (229). So not only are there insufficient professions open to women, but some are to be taken from them – midwives' jobs, she predicts, will go to men, men with a fancy French appellation, which no doubt makes them seem more professional and hence more trustworthy. This is particularly interesting in the light of the recent movement towards having only midwives present at birth, or, in some cases, *doulas*, trained birth-partners. Replacing midwives by male doctors does not just take a profession away from women, it also puts men in control of yet another aspect of women's lives. No wonder Wollstonecraft is displeased.

She continues to suggest that women 'might, also, study politics', that they could be put in charge of 'businesses of various kinds'. All these choices would be better, she says, than what is currently available, namely marrying for the sake of financial support, prostitution (which is a version of the same), or joining the thousands of women ruining their eyesight sewing for a living, or – Wollstonecraft's own bugbear – choosing a profession that offers very few rewards of any kind, that of governess.

She is very clear that a woman must have a place in society, whether or not she is married, and that no-one should have to marry if they do not want to. Although she may feel that a mother who does not take care of her children does not deserve the title of citizen, she clearly does not believe that all women have a duty to become mothers. One wonders what she would have thought had she known it would one day be the case that fathers could look after babies while mothers went to work. It seems she would have applauded that, for she clearly does not believe that women's nature predisposes them solely for motherhood:

> How many women thus waste their life away the prey of discontent, who might have practised as physicians, regulated a farm, managed a shop, and stood erect, supported by their own industry, instead of hanging their heads surcharged with the dew of sensibility, that consumes the beauty to which it at first gave lustre ...
>
> (230)

Whatever Wollstonecraft believes about the duties of a mother, she clearly does not think that woman's nature stops at motherhood, and she strongly believes in women having a set of real alternatives to marriage. This is much more consistent with her claim that woman's first duty is to herself as a rational being.

GOOD PARENTING

When it comes to parenting, Wollstonecraft is as stern and unforgiving as a modern child-rearing guru might be. From the very birth of the child, Wollstonecraft expects mothers to do their duty – that duty which nature has devolved on them – and to do it well. Not as well as they can, just well. One may say that, at the time when she wrote this, Wollstonecraft had no idea what it was to be a mother. However, when she did have a child, she turned out to be pretty much the mother she entreated other women to be. It did seem to come naturally to her and, most of the time, she enjoyed it. Maybe, then, she defined motherhood according to the kind of mother she, rightly, expected to become. But we may still feel that she did not pay sufficient attention to the different kinds of experience of motherhood that could be had, and to the different ways in which women could respond to them.

Like Rousseau, Wollstonecraft was insistent that mothers should breastfeed their babies. Her stated reasons were both that she felt breastfeeding was essential for early bonding between mother and child, and that the alternative – farming out one's children to wet-nurses – was simply not healthy. Wollstonecraft was well aware that the diet and lifestyle of a woman affected the quality of her milk. While a mother would take care to be healthy for the sake of the child she was feeding, a nurse probably wouldn't. In her letters from Sweden, she even suggests that the wet-nurse's unchaste habits could harm the infant by passing on venereal diseases (Wollstonecraft and Godwin 1987: 82).

In *A Vindication*, she goes as far as to argue that mothers must breastfeed in order to preserve their children from vice:

> Her parental affection, indeed, can scarcely deserve the name, when it does not lead her to suckle her children, because the discharge of

this duty is equally calculated to inspire maternal and filial affection: and it is the indispensable duty of men and women to fulfil the duties which give birth to affections that are the surest preservative against vice. Natural affection, as it is termed, I believe to be a very faint tie, affections must grow out of the habitual exercise of a mutual sympathy; and what sympathy does a mother exercise who sends her babe to a nurse, and only takes it from a nurse to send to school?

(234)

Receiving real affection from one's parents is a good way of not becoming vicious, she says. Presumably she believes that someone who is loved as a child will not be desperately seeking pleasure as an adult – and failing to find it – in vicious practices. This makes a certain amount of sense. But what is more difficult to accept is her linking of women feeding their infants to the giving of affection. In fact, in the context of eighteenth-century parenting practices, Wollstonecraft's concerns are not so difficult to understand. It would have been fairly common in the eighteenth century for a well-off mother to send her babies to live with a wet-nurse, not to see them till they were three years old, and then to spend very little time with them, preferring to leave them to the care of servants until they were old enough – particularly if they were boys – to be sent to school. So not feeding one's babies, in many cases, would amount to refusing to give them affection. Mothers, if they cared, would make the mistake of relying on the natural bond between themselves and their child, and be surprised, eighteen years later, to find themself facing a polite but cold stranger. So Wollstonecraft is probably not attacking women who do not breastfeed as such. In particular, she would probably be understanding of women who, for one reason or another, end up feeding their baby from a bottle.

It is not clear that women should feel threatened by Wollstonecraft's condemnation of eighteenth-century aristocratic child-rearing practices. These were particularly barbarous and had little to do with what working mothers nowadays choose to do. But, just in case we are still worried that sexism may be at work in an important way in Wollstonecraft's ideas on the rearing of infants, let us take a look at what she says about the role of men.

Men too, she says, must provide affection for their children, even if only indirectly by not preventing their wives from suckling:

> Besides there are many husbands so devoid of sense and parental affection, that during the first effervescence of voluptuous fondness, they refuse to let their wives suckle their children.
>
> (144)

And again:

> Cold would be the heart of a husband, were he not rendered unnatural by early debauchery, who did not feel much delight at seeing his child suckled by its mother.
>
> (223)

But the father must also be present, at least when they're not at work. And they should provide not only maintenance but social respectability to all their offspring, even illegitimate ones if they happen to have any (142). More importantly, Wollstonecraft says right at the beginning of the book:

> till men become more attentive to the duty of a father, it is vain to expect women to spend that time in the nursery which they 'wise in their generation' choose to spend at their glass.
>
> (68)

And the first step required towards fulfilling that duty, she says, is to refrain from a lifestyle that will 'weaken his constitution and debase his sentiments, by visiting the harlots'. There is a faint smell of eugenics behind that particular requirement, as Wollstonecraft tells us later that the children of parents who have contracted diseases through libertinage tend to be unhealthy:

> [T]he rich sensualist, who has rioted among women, spreading depravity and misery, when he wishes to perpetuate his name, receives from his wife only an half-formed being that inherits both its father's and mother's weakness.
>
> (218)[1]

It is fair to say, I think, that Wollstonecraft was strongly of the opinion that effective parenting had to be co-parenting. Men and women come together as parents, she says. This is where true marital affection is formed, in the joint love and concern parents feel for their offspring. There is no better illustration of what Wollstonecraft had in mind than the text she wrote for her own daughter, in which she describes the interaction of a child with her parents. This text, published by Godwin under the title 'Lessons' in 1798, was written either as a legacy for her first daughter before one of her suicide attempts, or when she was pregnant with her second daughter. Either way, she did not have time to finish it. The lessons consist first of words to learn and simple acts of hygiene and social interactions. Later, they place great emphasis on the development of reasoning skills. But they always reflect Wollstonecraft's idea of what a family should be like: one in which the parents love, respect and help each other. When the mother is working, or has a headache, the child is taught to seek her father, and to ask him, quietly, to play ball in the garden. When the father is sick, or asleep, the child comes with her mother to bring him camomile tea, or tiptoes and whispers so as not to wake him. What Wollstonecraft describes here seems like a very modern relationship, in which parents are equally concerned about the development and wellbeing of their child, as well as each other's wellbeing.

What this short text also illustrates well is Wollstonecraft's concern, apparent throughout *A Vindication*, that children should be educated to listen to reason. In her Chapter Two, she tell us that, although children must obey, this is only while their reason is growing. 'Till it arrives at some degree of maturity, you must look up to me for advice – then you ought to *think*, and only rely on God' (85). But this is advice a governess gives the children she teaches. What of parents? Does the same apply to them? It seems she is rather harsher:

> [F]or the absurd duty, too often inculcated, of obeying a parent only on account of his being a parent, shackles the mind, and prepares it for a slavish submission to any power but reason.

(236)

And again: 'A slavish bondage to parents cramps every faculty of the mind' (237). She goes on to say that to force daughters to obey is but a preparation for 'the slavery of marriage' (237), and that 'it is the irregular exercise of parental authority that first injures the mind, and to these irregularities girls are more subject than boys' (239).

She is right to suggest that it is never too early to form good thinking habits: children ought to be led to understand that they are rational creatures, and ought to be shown what rational creatures do. But it seems a little excessive (to say the least) to demand that parents never simply demand obedience without being prepared to give a rational explanation, or even work one out. Consistency, especially when one has several children, is, as every parent knows, extremely difficult to sustain. Parents usually find themselves having to make the best decision they can concerning a particular child, and may not always be a in a position to give a full account of why that decision is best. It will be based on their overall perception of the child's temperament, their needs, their situation, as well as principles they wish to apply to all their children. The result is bound to be that different restrictions are placed on different children. Parents will probably not be able to offer a fully rational explanation of the difference, and in any case, they will not be able to do so in a way that will satisfy their children's fledgling rational powers. At the end of the day, the only thing to say is probably 'Just do as I say!'.

That the burden Wollstonecraft places on parents to be consistent and appeal to their children's reason, or else be disobeyed, is especially clear when we consider that not all parents have as great a command of their rational powers as Wollstonecraft did. Some are poorly educated, some are simply not that clever. Should the children of these parents be told that they must not obey? Maybe that is true to some extent. If a teenage girl is told that she must marry and not go to university, even though she is keen to carry on with her studies, it might make sense for a teacher to suggest that she should not obey her parents. Again, if a young child has particularly vicious parents who respond to what they perceive to be bad behaviour on a particular day with violence, it is appropriate for somebody to step in and interfere. But what needs to be interfered with is the violence, rather than the inconsistency.

The kind of obedience that is required of a young child is often very different from that which is required of a teenager. A child has to obey, most often for their own comfort and safety, and sometimes for somebody else's comfort and safety. A parent who tells a daughter 'don't do that!', just because she is making a lot of noise for little purpose, is not usually called upon to justify herself. It is fine just to give an order and expect it to be obeyed. Consider the parent who tells his son not to be unpleasant to another child. When asked to justify himself, the father who is not very articulate can say nothing more than 'because it's not a nice thing to do'. A father who could sit down and explain to his child why we should be nice to each other might do a better job. But should the child of the first father disobey? Would that child be better off if he disobeyed? It seems not.

BAD PARENTING

The latter point leads us naturally to Wollstonecraft's thoughts on bad parenting. She seems to divide bad parenting into two main groups – tyrannical parenting and indolent parenting. By tyrannical parenting, she means mostly the kind of parenting that by-passes reasonableness – parents who expect to be obeyed simply through affection, and parents who do not attempt consistency in their treatment of their children. This type of parenting, she tells us, leads to children whose minds are 'shackled', who are unable to reason for themselves, but also to children who become tyrannical in their own right, having learned early on that to behave inconsistently and according to one's mood is acceptable.

> To elude this arbitrary authority girls very early learn the lessons which they afterwards practice on their husbands; for I have frequently seen a sharp-faced little miss rule a whole family, excepting that now and then mamma's anger will burst out of some accidental cloud; either her hair was ill-dressed, or she had lost more money at cards, the night before, than she was willing to own to her husband; or some such moral cause of anger.

(239)

Children cannot, she says, acquire respect for arbitrary parents, as children are rational creatures and will understand that some behaviour is not worthy of respect. Again, we need to take this with a pinch of salt – parents are often inconsistent, and children still (mostly) respect them. Whether or not they would have more respect for parents who were never inconsistent, we simply do not know and probably will never find out. But tyrannical parenting must be a matter of degree, and parents must be allowed sometimes to be less than fully consistent in their treatment of children without worrying that they will damage the development of their children's reasoning abilities.

The second category of parenting is specifically one that is found among aristocrats:

> The indolent parent of high rank may, it is true, extort a shew of respect from his child, and females on the continent are particularly subject to the views of their family who never think of consulting their inclination, or providing for the comfort of the poor victims of their pride. The consequence is notorious; these dutiful daughters become adulteresses, and neglect the education of their children, from whom they, in their turn, exact the same kind of obedience.
>
> (237)

Again, the objection is that the parents do not bother to treat their children as reasonable beings. Here they are merely ornaments, pretty things that can be given a few accomplishments and otherwise left to grow wild, merely to be admired.

Reading this passage, one again suspects that Jane Austen had read Wollstonecraft, and that she very much had such a picture of parenting in mind when she described the Bertrams in *Mansfield Park*.[2] Maria and Julia Bertram are given a governess whose job is to make sure they have all the accomplishments necessary for their rank. They are mostly ignored by their indolent mother and distant father, and spoiled by a prejudiced aunt. As adults, both fall for the libertine Henry Crawford. Maria marries a rich fool because Crawford turns her down, but a few months into the marriage, elopes with Crawford. At no point does she seem to have any sense that she is doing any wrong, that she oughtn't to be using people as she is, or even that she will only hurt herself though her actions. At the end of the novel, Austen shows Maria's and Julia's father, Sir Bertram, as contrite and finally realizing that his style of parenting was criminally negligent. He tries to make up for his failings by keeping a much closer eye on his younger daughter, Julia. But one suspects that it is too late, and that he will fall for the other extreme, that of tyrannical parenting.

At the end of Chapter Eleven, one is in part inclined to judge that Wollstonecraft, when she wrote *A Vindication*, knew very little of parenting, and that many of her remarks reflect her ignorance. It is good to remember, however, that when she did become a parent, she still insisted that parenting should always aim to develop a child's ability to reason for herself. This strikes her as obvious:

> few parents think of addressing their children in the following manner, though it is in this reasonable way that heaven seems to command the whole human race. It is your interest to obey me till you can judge for yourself; and the almighty Father of all has implanted an affection in me to serve as a guard to you while your reason is unfolding; but when your mind arrives at maturity, you must only obey me, or rather respect my opinions, so far as they coincide with the light that is breaking in your own mind.
>
> (237)

One can only respect such an attitude, even if one disagrees with the detail of how Wollstonecraft thinks it should be deployed.

9

CONCLUDING REFLECTIONS

A CONFLICTED ENDING

In the final two chapters of *A Vindication of the Rights of Woman*, Wollstonecraft goes back to the problems she raised in her Preface and Introduction – how can women be expected to be good wives and mothers if they are not educated? (Wollstonecraft 1999/ 1792: 71, 74). And what, practically speaking, should replace the 'false system of education' which renders women 'weak and wretched'?

In her Chapter Twelve, Wollstonecraft answers the second question in great detail, describing and justifying all aspects of a mixed, free-for-all (at least up to the age of nine) education. The schools she has in mind should be mixed not only to ensure that boys and girls receive the same education, but also so that they do not grow to erect a shroud of mystery around each other, but instead learn to know and respect each other and communicate with each other. This perfect picture of equality is spoiled somewhat towards the end of the chapter, when Wollstonecraft suggests that this form of education would prepare women for mother-hood. It seems that the equality she is defending does not completely penetrate the home: the duty of running a household and raising children still falls to women. In Chapter Thirteen, Wollstonecraft further explores the idea that women should be prepared for motherhood. She seems to be arguing that in order for a woman to be successful at motherhood, she must benefit from the same rights and education as men, and also that men must be good husbands and fathers. This raises the question as to how seriously she should be taken by feminist thinkers. Some might suspect that, far from preparing a revolution for women, Wollstonecraft is perpetuating patriarchal thinking, ensuring that any progress women's education undergoes first and foremost benefits men: educate women, and they will serve you better! Although one might suspect that this sort of argument is merely a clever way of presenting claims for equal rights to her sceptical readers, we must still find a way of understanding Wollstonecraft's insistence that it is natural for women to be mothers and that this is what they are being educated for. So there is definitely a conflict here, at least as far as the modern reader, who would like to see Wollstonecraft as a prototype of feminism, is concerned. This final chapter attempts to understand, if not to resolve, this conflict.

SCHOOL OF MORALITY

In Chapter Twelve, Wollstonecraft describes what, according to her, schools should be like. First of all, they should be day schools (247), as opposed to boarding schools, so that children receive the benefit both of a family upbringing, in which the growth of loyalty, love and honesty is encouraged, (246), and spend time every day among their peers, so they can develop their critical thinking skills and their natural curiosity through conversing freely (241). Second, the schools should be mixed (250). Wollstonecraft strongly believes that adult men and women will have healthier relationships, based on knowledge and respect of each other, if they are brought up together as children. Keeping them apart will only make a mystery of the 'other sex', which will then lead to artificial relationships based on ignorance and mistrust. Third, schools should be free for all (and compulsory) between the ages of five and nine, and there should be no segregation between rich and the poor, thereby creating social relations of mutual respect and equality (253). This is one of Talleyrand's recommendations. Like Wollstonecraft, he believed that the roots of democracy were better set at an early age, and that rich children who had sat on the school bench with poorer ones would find it harder to regard them as inferiors later in life, and a political relationship of equals would be a more likely outcome. The principle at work is the same as the one behind Wollstonecraft's insistence that boys and girls should be schooled together: if children learn to interact with each other, it is more likely that, as adults, they will be able to sustain relationships of mutual respect and friendship. The requirement that classes and sexes should mix is backed up by the suggestion that children should wear identical uniforms to school – rich and poor, boys and girls should come to learn in the same clothes (253). These clothes should be comfortable, as physical education, running freely in large, natural grounds, would be an important part of the curriculum. Wollstonecraft bemoans the practices she has witnessed in girls' and boys' schools alike that allowed children only to walk along alleys (not being allowed to step on the grass) and always paid attention to deportment, which meant they could not run freely, as children tend to (248).

In this chapter, as in previous ones, Wollstonecraft's concern for children's health is evident: she is saying that no class is so important that it should interfere with a child's time spent in the fresh air, taking free exercise. In her Chapter Four (132), Wollstonecraft had already explained that much of woman's condition was due to confinement in childhood and a lack of fresh air and exercise. Women are only fragile and weak, she said, because their bodies are not allowed to develop naturally. While their brothers play outside, they must stay indoors so as not to spoil their pretty dresses. Hence their dependence on men, their inability to claim their freedom and work towards independence, is owed partly to an artificially weakened body. If women were healthier and stronger, she suggests, they probably would not remain slaves long. In a recent article, philosopher of science Sharon Clough argues that there is in fact a link between increased hygiene and the incidence of asthma and other health problems, and that little girls, whose habits tend to be more closely supervised than little boys, suffer more from such complaints as a consequence (Clough 2010). Girls, she says, are not encouraged to play outside as they would run the risk of dirtying their pretty dresses. As a result, they do not pick up all the bacteria in the dust that would allow them to build immunities. Although Wollstonecraft is not familiar with the concept of bacteria, or immunity, it is clear that she believes that lack of exercise and lack of rough, unsupervised playing outdoors contributes to women's poor health, her keen powers of observation making up for her lack of relevant scientific knowledge, and putting her far ahead of her time.

Other requirements to fit in with the needs of children are that they should not be sitting in a classroom for longer than one hour at a time, and that alternative teaching methods should be sought. In particular, some topics would be better learned, she says, via Socratic conversations, including history and the human sciences (253). Wollstonecraft, as we saw in an earlier chapter, is vehemently opposed to rote learning: she believes that to make a small child recite a text he or she does not understand not only presents no benefit for the child, but also risks making that child arrogant, as he or she would be made to recite in public, and praised highly for their performance by adults who value appearance more than substantial learning (247).

Again, Wollstonecraft's ideas as to what a good school should be like are very much ahead of her time. In fact, what she proposes is not unlike, in many respects, the ideas of Maria Montessori, who claimed that a large degree of freedom within the school environment would help children discover their true nature and hence become better learners. But if Montessori schools, at least in theory, take in children up to the age of eighteen, Wollstonecraft's day schools stop at age nine. After this, children who are destined to go into service – that is, who would become servants in the households of richer people – move on to different, professional schools. Boys and girls are still together for the morning classes, but in the afternoons they are separated so as to learn specific skills pertaining to their future professions. So women will spend their afternoons learning how to sew, etc. Those who are either rich or talented will also move on to another school, where they will learn 'the dead and living languages, the elements of science, and continue the study of history and politics, on a more extensive scale, which would not exclude polite literature' (254). Note that Wollstonecraft does not question that higher education should be offered on grounds of wealth as well as talent. For all her outrage at hereditary power and arbitrary social distinctions, she still does not appear to find it problematic that wealth should determine who would stay on at school and who would not. Perhaps the idea of an educational system based purely on merit was inconceivable, not because she could not imagine the poor being educated – clearly she thought that if they were talented, they should stay on at school – but because she could not conceive of a rich family taking their children out of school before they had to, simply because they were not very clever.

In this second school for the rich and talented, boys and girls will still be together and will even take dance and music classes together (256). This would not lead to debauchery and the kind of libertinage and unchaste behaviour Wollstonecraft decries in adults because, she says, 'I presuppose that such a degree of equality should be established between the sexes as would shut out gallantry and coquetry, yet allow friendship and love to temper the heart for the discharge of higher duties' (254). Wollstonecraft asks if this may not encourage early marriage, and her answer, given what she previously had to say on the subject, is surprising. She says that early marriages are a good thing, that from them 'the most salutary physical and moral effects naturally flow' (254). Married men and women are less selfish, she says, and better suited for the duties of public life, than those who remain single. This is surprising considering her earlier distrust of early marriage as preventing women in particular from getting to know the world and enabling their knowledge to mature. However, in the context of an education that is as rich for men as for women, and in which women are not shielded from the world, Wollstonecraft's point makes more sense. In other words, early marriage is bad for women in the world Wollstonecraft actually knows, but were education to be reformed according to her recommendations, early marriage would be a good thing, and as a practice would contribute to the wellbeing of society as a whole, physical and moral.

Those secondary schools for the rich and talented last until the students 'come of age', until they can either get married or take up a profession. This means that, if they are to work, they must learn their trade while they are still in school. Wollstonecraft suggests that 'those who were designed for particular professions, might attend, three or four mornings in the week, the schools appropriate for their immediate instructions' (256). One might suppose she is referring here to men whose parents have chosen a profession for them, typically the clergy, the army, law or politics. Among the talented but less rich, one might expect that some men would become school teachers or private tutors, and the same may be true for women who do not expect to marry or inherit a private fortune. But we must remember that Wollstonecraft somewhat rebelled against the *status quo* as far as professions open to women were concerned. Women, she says in Chapter Nine, might be 'physicians, as well as nurses. And midwives [...] They might also study politics [...] Business of various kinds' (229). We can only suppose that Wollstonecraft still holds in Chapter Twelve that those professions should be open to women, and hence that 'those destined for particular professions' would mean something very different from what the context of eighteenth-century professional life would suggest, namely that only poor women were destined to work, and never at rewarding jobs. This seems to be borne out by something she says towards the end of Chapter Twelve: 'It is plain from the history of all nations, that women cannot be confined to merely domestic pursuits, for they will not fulfill family duties, unless their minds take a wider range [...]. Nor can they be shut out of the great enterprises' (260). However, a few pages earlier Wollstonecraft writes that enabling women to be interested in a wider range of subjects, in particular 'political and moral subjects', 'is the only way to make them properly attentive to their domestic duties' (255). She says this to support the point that engaging in so-called 'masculine pursuits' will not make women neglect their duties, so much as the 'indolence and vanity' which are typical traits of the fashionable woman. She concludes the chapter in very much the same vein when she says:

> The conclusion which I wish to draw, is obvious; make women
> rational creatures, and free citizens, and they will quickly become

good wives and mothers; that is – if men do not neglect the duties of husbands and fathers.

(265)

So there is no question that she is still defending equality. Women need rights and freedom, just like men. And men need to be good fathers and husbands, just like women need to be good mothers and wives. But it is nonetheless striking that in order to do so she feels she has to revert to domestic stereotypes, and remind the reader that women, no matter how educated, are still first and foremost mothers and wives, and suggest that the main reason for granting them rights is to enable them to fulfil their domestic duties better. This theme is carried through to the next chapter, so we will investigate it further in the coming section.

PECULIAR DUTY OF THEIR SEX

In her Chapter Ten, Wollstonecraft writes that 'the care of children in their infancy is one of the grand duties annexed to the female character by nature'. She reiterates this thought in Chapter Thirteen, when she says that 'the rearing of children [...] has justly been insisted on as the peculiar destination of woman' (278). Is it possible to discount these somewhat problematic claims as inessential parts of the argument, thinking that maybe Wollstonecraft is just paying lip-service to some of her readers, trying not to frighten them while still persuading them that women must have rights? This is certainly what her conclusion in Chapter Twelve suggests: women must be good wives and mothers, but they can only be that if they are full citizens, and the same applies to men, who must be good husbands and fathers. If that is all Wollstonecraft is saying, there is no reason to believe that her claims about the importance of motherhood threaten, in any way, the feminist position we want her to have.

Unfortunately, both in previous chapters and in the final chapter, Wollstonecraft makes claims which suggest that the duties of motherhood place rather more onerous demands on a woman's life than the duties of fatherhood place on a man's life. She seems to believe that it is part of a woman's nature to care for her children, so that she will only be fulfilled if she does so. Wollstonecraft then appears to adhere to a form of feminine essentialism – she believes that there is something fundamental in women's nature that makes them different from men. Typically, essentialism means that what we can become is, in part, determined by our nature, that we will not be successful members of our kind if we do not develop in certain ways. For Wollstonecraft, the essence of human nature is reason and the capacity to become virtuous. So to be a successful human being, one needs to use reason to acquire knowledge and virtue. And, although Wollstonecraft appears to believe that there is a female essence over and above this human essence, she is adamant that it is neither reason nor the capacity for virtue, which both belong to human nature and are genderless. Instead, she claims it is linked to women's physical nature: women are physically equipped to give birth to children and to breastfeed infants, and from this Wollstonecraft deduces that they have a naturally derived duty to do so. That she does not argue for this position may indicate that she has not spent a great deal of time analysing it or attempting to justify it. Rather, it may have struck her as obvious that as women could not help giving birth to babies once they were married, they had a duty to look after them.

What is interesting about Wollstonecraft's apparent feminine essentialism is that it is also teleological, in that she thinks women are designed to fare better if they are good mothers. For instance, breastfeeding means that women will be healthier and have less crowded families, as women are not fertile while they are breastfeeding and therefore cannot become pregnant again as soon as they have given birth. This is true, but there are exceptions and reservations. Breastfeeding is not the healthiest option for all women. It can be extremely painful and lead to children not feeding enough if they don't latch on properly. And while feeding a child for two years may ensure a space of nearly three years between each birth, this will place a burden on a woman's health, causing her, at the very least, to have backache, which will worsen with every child and make her household and childcare work more difficult and painful. Unfortunately, Wollstonecraft's ideal of the healthy, muscular woman cannot be realized for everyone: not all women have the same natural propensity towards health and strength, and some will suffer from giving birth and suckling their infants, no matter what Wollstonecraft tells us. She is also highly critical of aristocratic women's habits, such as drinking, and the diseases they have contracted through libertinage, which make them incapable of producing healthy milk for their children. But what would she say of women who are taking medication that prevents them from breastfeeding? Would her faith in nature's designs be shaken by this? It is hard to tell, but one can only surmise that she might be willing to revise some of her views, at least as far as allowing exceptions is concerned.

However, even more worryingly, Wollstonecraft does not trust nature to enforce its own rules, but believes that society should ensure nature's dictates are observed:

> I mean therefore to infer that the society is not properly organized which does not compel men and women to discharge their respective duties, by making it the only way to acquire that countenance from their fellow-creatures, which every human being wishes some way to attain.
>
> (222)[1]

This appears to entail that society should be so organized that a woman who chooses not to breastfeed her babies herself should be shunned by others. It is not entirely clear that Wollstonecraft believes that this should be legislated for, but given her reference to the proper organization of society, it is likely that she meant this. This way of thinking is obviously problematic from a feminist perspective, in that it puts women at a disadvantage by forcing them to use their bodies for the welfare of others for an extended period after each birth – as long as two years. Women of Wollstonecraft's time could not choose not to get pregnant if they were married, as contraception was neither reliable nor very much used. Wollstonecraft suggests that by breastfeeding infants they could make the intervals between pregnancies longer, but that means replacing one physically demanding job with another. In other words, Wollstonecraft is demanding of women that they perform a physically demanding job of the kind that their husband will never have to do, whether or not they choose to.

Wollstonecraft is not the only philosopher to believe that women should be forced to breastfeed. Aristotle, in Book VII of the *Politics* (which I have already suggested may have been an inspiration for some of Wollstonecraft's ideas), states that the lifestyle of pregnant women (diet and exercise) as well as the rearing of infants should be legislated for (1335b14–1336a1). More recently, philosophers have debated whether women should be obliged by law to breastfeed their children, contrasting women's right to choose how they use their body with the right of infants to receive the benefits of breast milk.[2] In some countries, this is actually legislated for, as for example in Indonesia, where women who do not breastfeed their children up to the age of six months face a fine of £7000. It is clear that Wollstonecraft's thoughts on this would not be rejected by all.

One reason why women nowadays might reject the claim that they have a duty to breastfeed their children is that this would be incompatible with their career. Women today do have alternatives to breastfeeding that do not involve sending their children away to live with a wet-nurse for two years. We can feed children formula milk specially designed to meet infants' nutritional requirements, or we can express our milk (provided our employer allows us sufficient time, comfort and privacy to do so) so that others can bottle-feed our children. These options simply did not exist in the eighteenth century.[3]

The question of how much responsibility for childcare should fall to the working mother is one that Wollstonecraft considers very little. In fact, she does not discuss in this respect the plight of working-class mothers, and has very little to say that would be useful for the modern working mother. One thing she does suggest, though, is that mothers may have the opportunity to engage in intellectually rewarding activities if they go about their duty well:

> And did they pursue a plan of conduct, and not waste their times in following the fashionable vagaries of dress, the management of their household and children need not shut them out from literature, nor prevent their attaching themselves to a science, with that steady eye which strengthens the mind, or practicing one of the fine arts that cultivate the taste.

(280)

In other words, whether or not mothers can work, they can become writers, scientists and artists. This presents a stark contrast to what was commonly regarded as suitable for a married woman – the exercise of accomplishments such as amateur drawing, painting and music. Women were expected to dabble in the arts, but not to become proficient. What Wollstonecraft is suggesting here is quite different, and is an interesting consequence of the requirement that women should be free and educated, but responsible for children and household. Once the children are old enough to go to school, a woman who has some help with housework will have more free time than her husband, who has to go out to work. She will, given her education, be able to use that time to conduct research, as any educated man of leisure would. In Wollstonecraft's world, the scientists, the artists and the writers will be women more often than men who, in this picture, have to work in order to earn a living. Nor is this simply idle speculation: when, a few years after writing *A Vindication*, she became a mother herself, Wollstonecraft carried on pursuing her career as a writer, producing both an account of the French Revolution, written according to research she conducted while residing in Paris during the Terror, and pregnant with her first child. Her letters from Sweden and Norway, published in 1796, were written during a trip she undertook to these countries on an expedition to investigate the loss of her lover's ship, accompanied by her toddler and a nanny. Wollstonecraft is right to insist that being a mother does not necessarily preclude producing work of distinction.

But Wollstonecraft does not take into account that some working mothers will have much less flexible lives, and no time for reading, let alone writing, because they will still be responsible for their household and childcare. Her picture of the savant mother belongs squarely to the middle and upper classes. A working-class mother who has to earn a living will never find the time for artistic, literary or scientific pursuits. And as Wollstonecraft informs us in Chapter Twelve, these women's formal education will have stopped at the age of nine, so they would be in no way prepared for such pursuits, even if they had the time for them. This exclusion is somewhat surprising, as Wollstonecraft seems very aware throughout the book of the plight of working women, and tends to praise them in comparison with middle-class women who could claim their freedom but choose to remain in their gilded cage. She knew from experience that working-class women had no time to devote to anything other than their work and family, having lived with the family of her friend Frances Blood, and observed how her friend and her mother worked from dawn till well into the night sewing and embroidering, just to make ends meet, and received no help financially or otherwise from the father who could not keep a job and did not regard it as his responsibility, as a man, to do household work. Wollstonecraft could not have expected women like this to become artists, writers or scientists.[4]

That Wollstonecraft does not recognize that motherhood means something very different for middle-class, aristocratic women on the one hand, and lower-class women on the other, means that she also probably cannot provide great insight on the condition of working mothers nowadays.[5] Women who have received a higher education nowadays tend not to decide to stay at home and look after their children while at the same time exercising their higher faculties by becoming artists, writers or scientists. Some do, of course, but in general neither women nor men feel that their intellectual life will be best fulfilled by becoming a scientist in their spare time. This is an eighteenth-century ideal that no longer operates. Scientists work in labs, not homes. Science is a profession, not a hobby.[6]

The way in which a lot of people do try and fulfil their intellectual life is through their professional life: people who have studied tend to want an interesting job that will engage them intellectually, force them to use the skills they have acquired and develop new ones, and present a challenge. It is often a complaint of mothers who end up staying at home to look after children that they do not find their lives challenging enough, that although they are sometimes hard, they are not interesting, consisting mostly of changing nappies, going to doctors' appointments, etc. Of course some women find that raising a child presents interesting challenges in itself. That was certainly the case for Wollstonecraft, who drew on her experiences with her first-born to write a manual of child-rearing. But Wollstonecraft was always fascinated with education – not everybody is, and many women may fail to be stimulated by a baby's daily progress. These women will probably long to go back to work, to an environment in which they can make use of the skills and abilities they have developed throughout their studies and early career. These women may, if they are lucky, find the fulfilment they seek by going back to work. But for many, no longer being able to look after their baby will cause them to feel guilty, if only because this is what society is expecting them to feel.

Some women choose to go back to work, but increasingly many women, from middle-class as well as working-class backgrounds, have no such choice: they have to go back to work in order to earn enough money to support their family. And this work is not always rewarding – so the fact that Wollstonecraft does not consider the plight of working mothers when she explains how fulfilling an educated mother's life may be is even more problematic as far as we are concerned. A large number of working mothers are not fulfilled, and have, somehow, to find the time and energy to care for their children and look after the house. Part of the answer to this problem is clearly that fathers need to take equal responsibility for household and childcare duties, and that we need to move away from Wollstonecraft's essentialist attribution of these duties to women. There is nothing natural about a couple coming home from a day's work, the man sitting down to read the paper while the woman cleans the house, puts the children to bed and prepares dinner – not unless we are prepared to think that women have vastly superior bodily strength than men, that is, we deny the one superiority Wollstonecraft grants that men have, and in fact reverse it. But there is no other way of explaining the attitude that, after a day's work, men need to rest but women must carry on working.

Another problem arising out of Wollstonecraft's thoughts on motherhood is that of childcare. Wollstonecraft is adamant, we saw, that women should not 'farm out' their children to nurses, both because it is healthier to breastfeed your baby yourself, and because you then miss out on the early years of your child's life, which, she says, following Locke and Rousseau, are extremely important for forming character. On the other hand, she does not appear to have any objection to other forms of help: she herself hired a full-time, live-in nanny to help look after her first daughter. Wollstonecraft would best be described, nowadays, as 'working from home'. As such, she was still able to spend a great deal of her time with her daughter and make sure that she was there to nurture and teach her. But her position, even taking into account that she was a single mother abandoned in France during the Terror, was somewhat privileged compared with that of most modern mothers. Very few women can afford to work from home and make enough money to employ a live-in nanny. The same is true of mothers who work part-time: they will find it hard to pay for the childcare needed to allow them to go to work. On the other hand, mothers who work full-time cannot, at the same time, be the primary care-giver in the home. Their children must be looked after by childminders, or go to nurseries. Because of the many differences between women's situation now and in the eighteenth century, nothing Wollstonecraft says seems to fit this picture. For her, the woman who does not raise her children herself misses out and cannot be fulfilled. But, at the same time, for an educated woman to be fulfilled, she must be engaged in some pursuits other than child-rearing and housework. We saw that the lofty eighteenth-century ideal of the stay-at-home mother scientist/artist was best translated as the thought that educated women often find fulfilment through an interesting career. However, unless one is independently wealthy, or married to a wealthy husband, work often means that a mother cannot be the primary care-giver for her children. If a mother chooses to stay at home rather than go out to work, on the other hand, she typically cannot engage in the kind of fulfilling activities Wollstonecraft suggests, because being a stay-at-home mother, without the luxury of hiring outside help, is a full-time job that leaves little time or energy for anything else. So Wollstonecraft is simply not helpful here. But, rather than accusing her of not being feminist enough, we should bear in mind that she could not have predicted how much women's condition would evolve in the 200 or so years after her death. We may suspect that she would even have revised her views on the naturalness of women raising children after witnessing men's abilities to be primary care-givers to babies and children. The possibility of feeding a baby from a bottle, whether formula or expressed milk, clearly did not, and could not have, come into her deliberations. Nor did she anticipate that, once society took seriously the idea she herself expressed that men should be brought up in an environment that nurtures rather than represses their emotions, they would become just as good at parenting infants and young children as women can be. Again, she may not have realized that her suggestion that women should take up a greater variety of professions meant they would be in a position to earn a sufficient income to provide for their family, so that it made sense, in at least some cases, for gender roles to be reversed, for fathers to stay at home and look after children while mothers went to work. Even if she had envisaged that the seeds she sowed would grow to such an extent, she might well not have wanted to share her vision with her audience, so as not to scare them off more than she had to.

AS ALL READERS ARE NOT SAGACIOUS ...

Is Wollstonecraft moderating her thoughts, even at times being deliberately misleading, because she wants to be influential? This is a vexed question, and one that she may not have been in a position to answer herself. In the Introduction, she offers a very puzzling statement to the effect that she will rely on the strength of her arguments, not the elegance of her words, to persuade. But that statement, and indeed the entire book, is formulated in a very elegant way indeed:

> Animated by this important project, I shall disdain to cull my phrases or polish my style; – I aim at being useful, and sincerity will render me unaffected; for wishing rather to persuade by the force of my arguments, than dazzle by the elegance of my language, I shall not waste my time in rounding periods, or in fabricating the turgid bombast of artificial feelings, which, coming from the head, never reach the heart. – I shall be employed about things, not words! – and, anxious to avoid that flowery diction which has slided from essays into novels, and from novels into familiar letters and conversation.

(74)

From this passage only, it seems that Wollstonecraft is being downright dishonest: she is using more adjectives and metaphors than she needs to in order to express her point.[7] Even taking into account that eighteenth-century writing did not tend towards minimalism, she is certainly less terse than Smith, for example. But could she have persuaded simply through the strength of her arguments? She admits herself that both men and women will be reluctant to hear the truth of what she has to say, that they will be eager to protect the lives and identities they have made for themselves, and that change, if it happens at all, will happen only slowly. She may well feel, under those circumstances, that a little deception or manipulation will not go amiss. Why not both present strong arguments and present them in a style that will give her readers more incentives to listen? Why not attempt to sweeten the pill?

In particular, this may mean that Wollstonecraft is not always honest about the extent to which she believes men and women are equal. Her emphasis on the 'physical superiority' of men in the early chapters, and her assurances that she does not want 'violently to agitate the contested question respecting the equality or inferiority of the sex' (72), are merely a preface to her very strong claim that men and women are equally rational and moral, and therefore should be equal as far as legal and political rights and duties are concerned in Chapter One.

This same ambivalence towards her readers, her desire to persuade them by appealing to their reason, while at the same time doubting that they have the rational abilities to engage with ideas as provoking as hers, is present also in her conclusion:

> It is not necessary to inform the sagacious reader, now I enter into my concluding reflections, that the discussion of this subject merely consists in opening a few simple principles, and clearing away the rubbish which obscured them. But as all readers are not sagacious, I must be allowed to add some explanatory remarks to bring the subject home to reason – to that sluggish reason, which supinely takes opinions on trust, and obstinately supports them to spare itself the labour of thinking.
>
> (280)

Short of calling her readers idiots, she tells them quite openly that their reason is probably not exercised enough to take in all she has to say, and that she should therefore repeat it, slowly, for their benefit. But she also tells us that what she has done is merely to clarify certain principles which had so far been obscured by prejudice. She does not claim to have exposed all the consequences that would follow from these principles. Had she done so more expressively, she would probably have found that her readership, instead of not being sagacious, was altogether nonexistent. So, for example, she says very little about what women's professions might be when they have been educated properly, preferring to expand on what the detail of this education should be. And she was successful to the extent that her work was well received – as a treatise on the education of women. But her purpose would have been well served had her educational advice been taken seriously for long enough – had her work not fallen into disrepute after the publication of her memoirs by her husband. Women who had received an education according to Wollstonecraft's specifications would then have been in a better position to demand a career for themselves.

This reasoning can be brought to bear on the questions raised at the end of the previous section. Should Wollstonecraft have known that it would become a new struggle of women to demand to go to work and leave their husbands to care for the home and babies, or at least to share these responsibilities – and any possible guilt about the placing of babies in nurseries – equally with them? No: Wollstonecraft should not have known all the twists and turns the feminist revolution would take. She put all her energy into starting it, by attempting to convince her contemporaries that women should receive an education equal to men, in the hope that this would eventually lead to equality of rights. Her suggestion that a properly educated eighteenth-century woman become a stay-at-home mother with the leisure to delve deeply into art and science, while her husband is busy earning the family's keep, is not detrimental to women: it is probably a plausible interpretation of what equality might mean for middle-class families in the late eighteenth century. It no longer works, but that is not something Wollstonecraft could have foreseen.

We cannot, probably, find in Wollstonecraft a handbook for twenty-first-century feminism. Unless we think nothing has changed since the eighteenth century, we should not even look for one. But this does not mean that we should strike her off the list of feminist philosophers, or even that we should regard her merely as a writer of historical interest for the feminist cause, but mostly redundant. Although her arguments are undoubtedly of historical interest, they are also strongly relevant to many issues with which we are still struggling today. As I have attempted to show throughout this book, some twenty-first-century problems would benefit from being looked at from Wollstonecraft's perspective, such as the plight of women in the developing world, who somehow do not think they need help; or the kind of attitude that regards rape victims as somehow responsible for the rape because they are 'unchaste'. Wollstonecraft's view on motherhood is the one aspect of her work a modern feminist might want to reject outright, but it is important to bear in mind that it is also the part of her work that is weakest from the point of view of philosophical rigour: she nowhere argues for the claim that women are essentially mothers, merely stating that it is widely accepted and therefore true. So we may want to reject this part of her work on philosophical as well as on feminist grounds. But this is not to say that her work as a feminist philosopher should not be prized – we do not refuse to read philosophers, or strike them from essential reading lists, on the grounds that they have a small number of bad arguments, or make a few claims for which they fail to argue. On such grounds, Aristotle and Kant, who make some wholly unsupported and strikingly offensive claims about women, should be struck out of reading lists everywhere. This is clearly not going to happen, and nor should it. But let us not hold Wollstonecraft to different standards simply because she is a woman. A few of her claims are unsupported, and probably would have been better not made – but that does not strip value from the rest of her work. We can, and probably should, as philosophers and feminists, take exception to her feminine essentialist claims – but that should not deter us from finding a great deal in her work to enrich our thinking and our general outlook. Her words remain an extremely valuable contribution to philosophy and feminist thought.

NOTES

1 THE FIRST OF A NEW GENUS

1 Mary grew up to become a writer herself. At seventeen, she eloped with Percy Shelley, then a married man. Her half-sister Fanny died of an overdose of laudanum at twenty-three, alone.

2 This was in part related to the culture of sensibility – it was, up to a point, expected of artistic or philosophical types that they should suffer in this way.

3 Her death, after the birth of her second daughter, was caused by an infection and had nothing to do with her robustness.

4 My emphasis (Wardle 1979: 164).

5 Indeed, many of these works were prefaced by an apology for breaching modesty by expressing oneself publicly, and giving the need for money as the reason for this breach (see Waters 2004: 415).

6 The French revolutionary Charlotte Corday, famous for murdering Marat in his bath, claimed at her trial that she had 'read everything'. Corday had been brought up by an uncle who left her to her own devices and did not lock the doors to his extensive library.

7 She did manage to teach herself enough French to translate French works into English, and to live for three years in France during the Revolution.

8 Because the Dissenters were excluded for religious reasons from attending English universities, they formed their own schools and colleges. Newington Green, where Wollstonecraft opened her second school, had several such academies, including Burgh's.

9 For an exposition of rational Dissent and its influence in eighteenth-century publishing, see Braithwaite (2003).

10 Locke's *Some Thoughts on Education* came out in 1693, Burgh's *Thoughts on Education* in 1747, and Wollstonecraft's *Thoughts on the Education of Daughters* in 1787.

11 She had planned to go with others, but the first trip was aborted due to news of violence in Paris. She undertook the second trip alone. Fuseli was married, but Wollstonecraft had suggested that since she and he were clearly soul-mates, they could set up a *ménage à trois* with his wife providing the physical side of the relationship, and Wollstonecraft the moral and intellectual side. The Fuselis, understandably, were not impressed.

12 By marrying her Godwin, too, risked his reputation – with both his friends and readers, as he had written explicitly against the institution of marriage, and with society at large, by marrying a woman who had previously lived in sin and had a child out of wedlock.

13 Suicide was then perceived as a sin, and there was a strong stigma attached to mental illness such as the depression that led Wollstonecraft to attempt suicide.

14 Although *A Vindication of the Rights of Woman* is what she was famous for, this was mostly read as a treatise on education.

15 The Todd and Butler edition contains some references to the text of the first edition (Todd and Butler 1989, Vol. 5).

16 In order to write the *Treatise of Human Nature*, David Hume retired to rural France for three years, while Kant's *Critique of Pure Reason*, although written in five months, was the product of twelve years' reflection and lecturing (see Quinton 1998: 6 and Scruton 1982: 7).

17 George Eliot's review essay 'Margaret Fuller and Mary Wollstonecraft' was first published in *The Leader* in 1855.

18 Harriet Taylor was Mill's friend, then wife. Mill claimed to owe many of his ideas to her, and this may be particularly true in the case of the *Subjection*. Taylor was already dead when Mill began to write the *Subjection* in 1860, and the help he acknowledges is that of her daughter, Helen Taylor.

19 There is evidence that Mill was at least made aware of Wollstonecraft, as Auguste Comte mentioned having read her to Mill in correspondence (Haac 1995: 188). However, Mill says nothing in his reply that suggests he has read, or wishes to read, *A Vindication*. Helen Taylor reports having read *A Vindication* as a teenager, and that the book was a gift from her mother. But this tells us nothing about when Harriet read it, nor whether she made anything of it philosophically.

20 Which is not to say that it does not still require a fair amount of work, or that there is no urgency in defending feminist practice.

2 THE RIGHTS OF WOMAN AND NATIONAL EDUCATION

1 Godwin published a series of notes along with other posthumous works. The title of the published notes was 'Hints [Chiefly designed to have been incorporated in the Second Part of the *Vindication of the Rights of Woman*]'. These notes do

not, however, pertain to legal matters regarding women's condition (Todd and Butler 1989, Vol. 5: 267–76).

2 Claudia Johnson suggests that *Maria* perhaps should not be regarded as fictionalized philosophy, but a novel in its own right. It is, however, possible that Wollstonecraft simply decided to express her thoughts outside philosophy (Johnson 2002: 189–208).

3 As for poorer women, she is probably assuming they do not buy books. This cannot be a blanket assumption, of course, as her friend Frances Blood came from a poor family but was very well read. She may have considered some working women, such as Frances and her mother, who was a seamstress, to belong to the lower middle classes.

4 Rousseau, as well as writing political and literary texts that came to be highly influential during the French Revolution, had written a large volume on education: *Emile* (referred to as *Emilius* by Wollstonecraft), in which he details the perfect education for a boy and for his wife-to-be, Sophie (or Sophia, in Wollstonecraft). Although Wollstonecraft admired many of Rousseau's thoughts on education, she did not share his views on the education of women.

5 As well as evidence of her admiration in the text of *A Vindication*, there is a long review of the letters Wollstonecraft wrote for the *Analytical Review* (Todd and Butler 1989, Vol. 7: 309–22).

6 She was not alone in having found educational writing a profitable niche: likewise popular were Madame de Genlis's stories and Dr Fordyce's *Sermons*, and Dr Gregory's *Legacy to his Daughters*, to name but a few. The popularity of the genre was helped by Wollstonecraft's publisher, Johnson, who made it his responsibility to encourage the proliferation of educational writings.

7 Wollstonecraft probably first read Rousseau under the guidance of the Clares, in her late teens. We know that she first read *Emile* in 1787, as she wrote about it to her sister (Wardle 1979: 145). We also know that by 1788, she had read enough of Rousseau that she could comment on the quality of a selection of extracts from his works (Todd and Butler 1989, Vol. 7: 49). At that time, she described him as an 'author thoroughly acquainted with the human heart', although she already saw 'paradoxes' in *Emile*. When in the summer of 1790 she reviewed Rousseau's *Confessions*, she still spoke of him as a genius, an honest and passionate man (*ibid.*: 228).

8 *A Female Reader* is discussed by Moira Ferguson in her article on the discovery of that previously lost anthology (Ferguson 1978).

9 John Adams, who became the second president of the United States, did not, of course, pay heed to his wife's demands. The Adams became good friends of Price during their stay in Europe, and Abigail Adams became an admirer of Wollstonecraft's work.

10 As a historian, Macaulay derived her notion of Republicanism from a tradition in which one must qualify for citizenship, through either property ownership, class or education.

11 Also Rousseau, for whom breaking away from arbitrary authority is probably the main motivation as far as republicanism is concerned.

12 She also appears to have been familiar with Kant's work on the Sublime and the Beautiful, as she refers to it in her *Hints* (Todd and Butler 1989, Vol. 5: 275).

13 Even though in 'What is Enlightenment?' Kant refers to women as being particularly in need of help in achieving maturity, in an early piece on the Sublime
and the Beautiful, Kant stated that a woman who knows Greek, or who writes
about science, might as well have a beard (Kant 1960/1764: 78).

14 I discuss Condorcet's views in Chapter Five.

3 BRUTES OR RATIONAL BEINGS?

1 On a Socratic understanding of the relation between reason and virtue, this
would not make sense: the Plato of the Socratic dialogue argues that it is
impossible to act reasonably and not virtuously. I think we may safely conclude
that Wollstonecraft would disagree with this view.

2 This is perhaps not the best reading of Gilligan, who does not explicitly reject the
value of reason anywhere. Instead, she claims that the female subjects of her
experiments choose to reason about things other than rights, which, according to
Kohlberg, is what moral reasoning ought to be about. As we will see in a later
chapter, her views are more complex than they are generally made out to be.

3 For a good discussion of the relationship between feminism and rationality, see
Heikes 2010.

4 Genevieve Lloyd, who discusses at length the seventeenth- and eighteenth-century construction of a male reason, alludes only very briefly to Wollstonecraft as
being 'exasperated' with Rousseau's claims about the female (lack of) reason
(Lloyd 1984: 76).

5 With the notable exception of Taylor (2003: 106), who argues that Wollstonecraft's feminism is motivated by religion, that she believes that women should
be educated for the sake of the love of God.

6 Although she started life as an Anglican, it is not clear whether she had any
particular denomination by the time she died. There is little evidence to suggest
whether she did so or not.

7 The first edition was not so carefully worded, and Wollstonecraft made a rather
bigger concession to male superiority then, as she said that the female 'in general,
is inferior to the male. The male pursues, the female yields – this is the law of
nature' (Todd and Butler 1989, Vol.5: 74, note 4). It is significant that she thought
better of this when she went on to revise her text for the second edition.

4 RELATIVE VIRTUES AND MERETRICIOUS SLAVES

1 We should probably especially not encourage them to take up these professions.
It is clearly better that bankers should be honest and soldiers in control of their
aggressivity.

2 See my book on this topic: Berges 2009.

3 The Scottish Enlightenment thinker John Gillies published his first translation of
the *Nicomachean Ethics* and the *Politics* in 1797. Prior to that, the *Ethics* and the
Politics were available only in Greek, or mostly Latin, and there was a 1598
translation of the *Politics* from the French presumed to be by John Donne.

4 Poster notes, however, that in Scotland there was already the beginning of an Aristotelian revival (Poster 2008: 385).

5 Natalie F. Taylor, in her excellent discussion of Aristotelianism and Lockeanism in Wollstonecraft, cites evidence that Wollstonecraft was familiar with at least some of the *Politics*. She points out that in her *Vindication of the Rights of Men*, Wollstonecraft challenges Burke by suggesting, rightly, that he is quoting a misleading extract from the *Politics*, where Aristotle says that a democracy has points in common with a tyranny (Taylor 2007: 8). This passage makes it plausible either that Wollstonecraft had access to the 1598 translation of the *Politics*, or that she had taken part in some extensive discussions of this text with her more learned friends. This would not have made her an expert on Aristotle, but certainly she would have been conversant with his arguments.

6 See Berges (2009).

7 See her discussion of this in her Chapter Twelve, 'On national education'.

8 Wollstonecraft discusses Gregory's Legacy to his Daughters in some detail in Section III of her Chapter Five: Animadversions. We will consider her discussion in Chapter Six of this book.

9 This is one occasion where we might well suspect a neo-Platonist influence, which could have come from Price.

10 Taylor (2007: 141) makes this point very well.

11 Wollstonecraft, at this point in her life, had very little positive to say about the passions. She had suffered from unrequited love, had witnessed what disasters unions between men and women could bring about, and suffered from several bouts of depression which interfered with her work. Later, when he was writing her biography, her husband referred to her as a female Werther – a very passionate being who is made terribly unhappy by their passions.

12 She herself almost certainly experienced homosexual love for her friend Fanny Blood, so much so that her husband referred to her as a 'young Werther'. That was dignified, not because it was not consummated (her friend was engaged to a man and presumably straight), but because it was a meeting of equals who respected each other's the humanity.

13 See for example Samira Bellil's (2008) account of what it is like to be a young woman in a Parisian suburb.

14 In 2011, women throughout the world still earn less than men for similar work: See the *Global Gender Gap Report 2011*: www.weforum.org/women-leaders-and-gender-parity

5 ABJECT SLAVES AND CAPRICIOUS TYRANTS

1 Out of over sixty uses of 'slavery' and related words in *A Vindication*, only one refers to African slaves:

> Is one half of the human species, like the poor African slaves, to be subject to prejudices that brutalize them [...]?

(225)

2 If sensibility is a sickness of the times, it is not, Wollstonecraft tells us, one that is unique to women. 'Men and women should not have their sensations heightened in the hot-bed of luxurious indolence, at the expense of their understanding; for unless there be a ballast of understanding, they will never become either virtuous or free: an aristocracy, founded on property or sterling talents, will ever sweep before it, the alternately timid, and ferocious, slaves of feeling' (140). Quoting a translation of Voltaire by Adam Smith, Wollstonecraft directs us to the effeminate character of aristocratic men, following the example of Louis XIV who 'surpassed all his courtiers in the gracefulness of his shape, and the majestic beauty of his features' (129). Aristocrats impress, she and Smith agree, not through their virtue, their intellect or even their physical prowess, but merely through 'frivolous accomplishments' (129).

3 cf. Sapiro (1992: 227).

4 Translated by John Morley as 'Condorcet's plea for the citizenship of women' in Pyle (1995).

5 The 'hot-bed' Wollstonecraft refers to (140) was the eighteenth-century equivalent of the hot-house, a pit filled with horse manure and covered with glass.

6 Barbauld is quoted in a footnote in Chapter Four of *A Vindication* (123). Burke (1990: 105–6) compares women's beauty to the 'delicate myrtle'. The reference to Pope is to Butt (1968: 561): 'Epistle II, To a Lady (of the Characters of Women)'. The line from Swift is from 'The Lady's Dressing Room' (Rogers 1983: 452). Rousseau's advice to lady gardeners is in his *Letters on the Elements of Botany Addressed to a Lady* (Martyn 1787: 28). For an insightful discussion of gardening analogies in the eighteenth century, see George (2005).

7 Jon Elster (1985) emphasizes that the phenomenon of sour grapes is causal rather than intentional. It is not the case, in the examples discussed by Sen and Nussbaum, that people choose to deal with disappointment by forcing themselves to forget about it – it is an unconscious process.

8 For references to Wollstonecraft, see Sen (2006, 2009).

6 ANGELS AND BEASTS

1 The *Theodicy*, the *New Dialogues* and the *Animadversiones in Partem Generalem Principiorum Cartesianorum*.

2 Three republican pamphlets attacking monarchy and justifying regicide.

3 Blake, who illustrated Wollstonecraft's *Original Stories from Real Life* also illustrated Milton.

4 My translation.

5 Madame de Stael is reputed to have written a large part of Talleyrand's pamphlet on educational reform. If that is so, then it confirms Wollstonecraft's suspicions that she was a highly intelligent, powerful woman who worked hard at ensuring women did not acquire equal rights.

6 Barbauld's poem 'To a lady, with some painted flowers' attracted Wollstonecraft's critique in her Chapter Four (123). Barbauld replied with another poem, 'The Rights of Woman', in which she paints a doomed attempt by a woman to achieve equal rights, and her return to her natural position as a lover (Craciun

2002: 41). Barbauld did not publish the poem until after Wollstonecraft's death, even though she wrote it immediately after the publication of *A Vindication*. William McCarthy suggests that, rather than an attempt at refuting Wollstonecraft's arguments, the poem could be read as a retraction or a self-correction, that Barbauld is saying of herself 'I was a foolish Rousseauist myself!' (McCarthy 2008: 353).

7 Amy Goodman once gave a public lecture entitled 'Mary Wollstonecraft, the pioneer of modern womanhood'.

8 Wollstonecraft (1994: 69; 1999/1792: 229). Brace (2000: 435) claims that Wollstonecraft bases duties of men and women on natural division of labour, and that therefore motherhood holds an important place in virtuous womanhood. This seems less persuasive in the light of the passages I quoted in which Wollstonecraft describes what a woman might and should do.

8 RATIONAL FELLOWSHIP OR SLAVISH OBEDIENCE?

1 Could she have been aware of the effects of syphilis on reproduction? These were not recognized by the medical profession until the early twentieth century, and even then they were not widely publicized, to protect men from having to advertise the fact that they had been with prostitutes either before or during their marriage. Wives became sick, and gave birth to babies who were either still-born or lived, painfully, for a couple of years. Women were told that it was their inability to produce strong offspring that was to blame, whereas it was in fact an effect of the syphilis contracted by their husband. The American feminist writer Charlotte Perkins Gilman attempted to make this phenomenon more widely known in 1910 by publishing a novel, *The Crux*, in which she describes the effects of syphilis on marriage and reproduction, and in which the heroine is advised against marriage to a repented syphilitic because she would harm the 'national stock' by giving birth to unhealthy children. Gilman had access to recent medical research on this topic. The bacteria that causes syphilis had been discovered in 1905, and Gilman had sufficient medical background to understand the implications of the new discoveries. Wollstonecraft, although she counted Priestley, an innovator in medical thought, among her close friends, did not have access to this kind of knowledge. But it is possible, at least, that she may have guessed that there was a link between libertinage and diseased offspring.

2 Several writers have argued that Austen did in fact read Wollstonecraft, on the ground that she appears to endorse many of her views, and at various places in her novel seems to be borrowing from the characters in Wollstonecraft's novels. She did not, however, ever refer to her by name. See for instance Mellor (2002: 156) and Tauchert (2007: 221).

9 CONCLUDING REFLECTIONS

1 She adds on the same page that 'Nature has wisely attached affection to duties to sweeten toil, and to give that vigour to the exertions of reason which only the heart can give.'

2 For instance, see discussion in Roache (2010).

3 The extraction of breast milk through mechanical pumps or by hand became a recognized practice for feeding infants in the mid-nineteenth century (Lepore 2009).

4 Yet her friend Frances Blood was an artist, and made part of her living by selling botanical drawings. But this was hand-to-mouth living, and she did not have the leisure to experiment with her art, working only on what she sold.

5 'She also fails to recognize that the tensions between motherhood and citizenship affect middle-class and working-class women in different ways' (Brace 2000: 435).

6 The same is true for art and literature: neither is generally considered as hobbies one exercises in one's spare time. There are exceptions: best-selling writer Stephenie Meyer claims the idea for the *Twilight* book series came to her in a dream, and that she worked out the plot 'between swimming lessons and potty training', writing it out late at night when everyone was asleep. But she herself probably would not describe her works as great literature. And she would certainly not claim that this is a reliable way of producing works of art. Her example is perhaps one of how inspiration can strike in the most unlikely circumstances, and how determination can overcome the greatest obstacles. But it is quite clear that nobody in their right mind would choose motherhood as a way into literature, art or science.

7 'Turgid', for instance, means very much the same as 'bombastic'. Hence it is redundant in the expression 'turgid bombast'.

BIBLIOGRAPHY

Baier, A. (1994) *Moral Prejudices: Essays on Ethics*, Cambridge, MA: Harvard University Press, pp. 1–17.

Bellil, S. (2008) *To Hell and Back*, Lincoln, NE: University of Nebraska Press.

Berges, S. (2009) *Plato, Virtue and the Laws*, London: Continuum.

Brace, L. (2000) '"Not empire but equality": Mary Wollstonecraft, the marriage state and the sexual contract', *Journal of Political Philosophy*, 8: 33–455.

Braithwaite, H. (2003). *Romanticism, Publishing and Dissent: Joseph Johnson and the Cause of Liberty*, Basingstoke: Palgrave Macmillan.

Burke, E. (1968) *Reflections on the Revolution in France*, Harmondsworth: Penguin.

——(1990), *A Philosophical Enquiry into the Origins of our Ideas of the Sublime and the Beautiful*, Oxford: Oxford University Press.

Butt, J. (ed.) (1968) *The Poems of Alexander Pope*, London: Routledge.

Clough, S. (2010) 'Gender and the hygiene hypothesis', *Social Science & Medicine*, 72(4): 486–93.

Cobbe, F.P. (1869/1995) 'The subjection of women', in Pyle, A. (ed.), *The Subjection of Women*, Bristol: Thoemmes Press, pp. 54–74.

Craciun, A. (2002) *Mary Wollstonecraft's A Vindication of the Rights of Woman, A Sourcebook*, London: Routledge.

Darley, J.M. and Batson, C.D. (1973) 'From Jerusalem to Jericho: a study of situational and dispositional variables in helping behavior', *Journal of Personality and Social Psychology*, 27: 100–8.

Elster, J. (1985) *Sour Grapes: Studies in the Subversions of Rationality*, Cambridge: Cambridge University Press.

Fergusson, M. (1978) 'The discovery of Mary Wollstonecraft's *The Female Reader*', *Journal of Women in Culture and Society*, 3(4): 945–57.

George, S. (2005) 'The cultivation of the female mind: enlightened growth, luxuriant decay, and botanical analogy in eighteenth century texts', *History of European Ideas*, 31: 209–23.

Gilligan, C. (1982) *In a Different Voice*, Cambridge, MA: Harvard University Press.

——(1997) 'Voice and relationship: rethinking the foundations of ethics', Ethics Across the Curriculum, University of San Diego, 30 January. http://ethics. sandiego.edu/video/Gilligan/Lecture/Voice_and_Relationship.html

Gordon, L. (2006) *Vindication: A Life of Mary Wollstonecraft*, New York: Harper Perennial.

Haac, O. (trans.) (1995) *The Correspondence of John Stuart Mill and Auguste Comte*, New Brunswick, NJ: Transaction Publishers.

Heikes, D. (2010) *Rationality and Philosophy*, London: Continuum.

Hume, D. (2007) 'Of the standard of taste', in *Essays: Moral, Political and Literary*, New York: Cosimo Classics.

Janes, R.M. (1978) 'On the reception of Mary Wollstonecraft's A Vindication of the Rights of Woman', *Journal of the History of Ideas*, 39: 293–302.

Johnson, C. (ed.) (2002) *The Cambridge Companion to Mary Wollstonecraft*, Cambridge: Cambridge University Press.

Jones, E.E. and Harris, V.A. (1967) 'The attribution of attitudes', *Journal of Experimental Social Psychology*, 3: 1–24.

Kant, I. (1960/1764) *Observations on the Feelings of the Beautiful and the Sublime*, Goldthwait, J. (trans.), Berkeley, CA: University of California Press.

Kaplan, C. (2002) 'Mary Wollstonecraft's reception and legacies' in Johnson, C. (ed.), *The Cambridge Companion to Mary Wollstonecraft*, Cambridge: Cambridge University Press, pp. 246–70.

Kohlberg, L. (1981) *Essays on Moral Development*, San Francisco, CA: Harper and Row.

Lepore, J. (2009) 'Baby food', *The New Yorker*, 19 January, www.newyorker.com/ reporting/2009/01/19/090119fa_fact_lepore

Lloyd, G. (1984) *The Man of Reason, 'Male' and 'Female' in Western Philosophy*, Minneapolis, MN: University of Minnesota Press.

Macaulay, C. (1996/1790) *Letters on Education*, London: William Pickering.

Martyn, T. (trans.) (1787) *Rousseau, Letters on the Elements of Botany Addressed to a Lady*, London: B.White and Sons.

McCarthy, W. (2008) *Anna Letitia Barbauld: Voice of the Enlightenment*, Baltimore, MD: Johns Hopkins University Press.

McKeon, R. (ed.) (1941) *The Basic Works of Aristotle*, New York: Random House.

Mellor, A.K (2002) 'Mary Wollstonecraft's A Vindication of the Rights of Woman and the women writers of her day', in Johnson, C. (ed.), *The Cambridge Companion to Mary Wollstonecraft*, Cambridge: Cambridge University Press, pp. 141–59.

Micheli, G. (2005) 'The early reception of Kant's thought in England 1785–1805', in MacDonald Ross, G. and McWalter, T. (eds), *Kant and his Influence*, London: Continuum.

Mill, J.S. (1989) *On Liberty and Other Writings*, Cambridge: Cambridge University Press.

Morley, J. (trans.) (1995) 'Condorcet's plea for the citizenship of women', in Pyle, A. (ed.), *The Subjection of Women, Contemporaries' Responses to John Stuart Mill*, Bristol: Thoemmes Press.

Palmer, R.P. (1985) *The Improvement of Humanity. Education and the French Revolution*, Princeton, NJ: Princeton University Press.

Pettit, P. (1999) 'Republican freedom: contestatory democratization', in Shapiro, I. and Hacker-Gordon, C. (eds), *Democracy's Value*, Cambridge: Cambridge University Press.

Pitcher, E. (1975) 'The serial publication and collecting of pamphlets 1790–1815', *Transactions of the Bibliographical Society*, 30(4): 323–29.

Poster, C. (2008) 'Whose Aristotle? Which Aristotelianism? A historical prolegomenon to Thomas Farrell's norms of rhetorical culture', *Philosophy and Rhetoric*, 41(4): 377–401.

Price, R. (1994/1787) *Review of the Principal Questions in Morals*, Cheltenham: Nelson Thornes/Classworks.

Pyle, A. (1995) *The Subjection of Women*, Bristol: Thoemmes Press.

Quinton, A. (1998) *Hume*, London: Phoenix.

Reiss, H.S. (ed.) (1991) *Kant's Political Writings*, Cambridge: Cambridge University Press.

Roache, R. (2010) 'Is it criminal not to breastfeed?', *Practical Ethics*, http://blog.practicalethics.ox.ac.uk/2010/08/is-it-criminal-not-to-breastfeed

Rogers, P. (ed) (1983) *Swift: The Complete Poems*, Harmondsworth: Penguin.

Rousseau, J.-J. (1992) *Emile ou de l'Education*, Paris: Bordas.

Ryle, G. (1966/2009) 'Jane Austen and the moralists', in Ryle, G. (ed.), *Collected Papers Vol. 1*, London and New York: Routledge, pp. 286–301.

Sapiro, V. (1992) *A Vindication of Political Virtue*, Chicago, IL: University of Chicago Press.

Scruton, R. (1982) *Kant*, Oxford: Oxford University Press.

Sen, A. (1992) *Inequality Re-examined*, Cambridge, MA: Harvard University Press.

——(2006) 'Reason, freedom, and well-being', *Utilitas*, 18: 80–86.

——(2009) *The Idea of Justice*, Harmondsworth: Penguin.

Springborg, P. (ed.) (1997) *Mary Astell, A Serious Proposal to the Ladies (1694 and 1697)*, London: Pickering and Chatto.

Stohr, K. (2006) 'Manners, morals and practical wisdom', in Chappell, T. (ed.), *Values and Virtues*, Oxford: Oxford University Press, pp. 189–211.

Tauchert, A. (2007) '*Pride and Prejudice*: Lydia's gape', in Bloom, H. (ed.), *Jane Austen's Pride and Prejudice: Critical Interpretations*, New York: Infobase Publishing.

Taylor, B. (2003) *Mary Wollstonecraft and the Feminist Imagination*, Cambridge: Cambridge University Press.

Taylor, H. (1851/1995) 'The enfranchisement of women', in Pyle, A. (ed.), *The Subjection of Women*, Bristol: Thoemmes Press, pp. 11–36.

Taylor, N.F. (2007) *The Rights of Woman as Chimera*, New York: Routledge.

Taylor, T. (1792/1996) *A Vindication of the Rights of Brutes*, Ann Arbor, MI: Scholars' Facsimiles & Reprints.

Thompson, W. (with Doyle Wheeler, A.) (1825) *Appeal of One Half of the Human Race, Women, against the Pretensions of the Other Half, Men*, London: Longman, Hurst, Rees, Orme, Brown and Green.

Todd, J. and Butler, M. (1989) *The Works of Mary Wollstonecraft*, in seven volumes, London: William Pickering.

Wardle, R. (ed.) (1979) *Collected Letters of Mary Wollstonecraft*, Ithaca, NY: Cornell University Press.

Waters, M. (2004) 'The first of a new genus: Mary Wollstonecraft as a literary critic and mentor to Mary Hays', *Eighteenth Century Studies*, 37: 415–34.

Wollstonecraft, M. (1994) *Thoughts on the Education of Daughters*, 1787, Oxford: Woodstock Books.

——(1999) *A Vindication of the Rights of Woman (1792), A Vindication of the Rights of Men (1790)*, Oxford: Oxford University Press.

Wollstonecraft, M. and Godwin, W. (1987) *A Short Residence in Sweden and Memoirs of the Author of 'The Rights of Woman'*, Harmondsworth: Penguin.

Woolf, V. (1965/1932) 'Mary Wollstonecraft', reprinted in Woolf, V., *The Second Common Reader*, London: Hogarth Press.

INDEX